Table of Contents

Steps for Learning Spelling Words

1. Look carefully at the spelling word.

2. Say the spelling word out loud.
   • How many syllables do you hear?
   • What consonant sounds do you hear?
   • What vowel sounds do you hear?

3. Check the word for spelling patterns.

4. Spell the word out loud.

5. Cover the spelling word.

6. Write the spelling word from memory.

7. Check the spelling word.

8. Repeat as needed.

Say each word out loud. Listen for the short *a* sound.

Copy and spell each word three times using colours of your choice.

1. lavender _____ _____ _____

2. forecast _____ _____ _____

3. cactus _____ _____ _____

4. Italy _____ _____ _____

5. abacus _____ _____ _____

6. elasticity _____ _____ _____

7. graphic _____ _____ _____

8. bamboo _____ _____ _____

9. discard _____ _____ _____

10. hyena _____ _____ _____

Brain Stretch

- Create a word search puzzle based on the spelling words.
- On a piece of paper, write a sentence using each spelling word.

abacus	bamboo	cactus	discard	elasticity
forecast	graphic	hyena	Italy	lavender

1. Fill in the blank using the best spelling word from the list.

a) My mom keeps dried _____ in all our closets to keep them fresh.

b) I like to read _____ novels because they are like comic books.

c) In the desert in Arizona, we saw a very tall and spiky _____.

d) The weather _____ said it will be hot and sunny tomorrow.

e) The _____ of stretchy pants is a lot greater than blue jeans.

f) I'm learning to do math on an _____. It's fun!

g) My Uncle Charlie sounds like a _____ when he laughs!

h) Always make sure you _____ food waste in the compost bucket.

i) My grandparents are my Nonna and Nonno. They are from _____.

j) The giant panda's favourite food is _____.

Brain Stretch

How many spelling words can you fit into one sentence and still make sense?
Give it a try!

1. Underline the word that is spelled incorrectly.

   a) graffic   graphic   b) hyena   hyeena

   c) abackus   abacus   d) Italy   Ittallee

   e) forecast   forkast   f) cacktus   cactus

   g) bamboo   bhambou   h) lahvendur   lavender

2. Unscramble the spelling word. Write the word on the line.

   a) lyait _____   b) baascu _____   c) yneah _____

   d) obmboa _____   e) scfaerto _____   f) ascctu _____

   g) hpcargi _____   h) rdanveel _____

3. Circle the word with the short *a* sound that makes the most sense.

   Write the word in the sentence.

   a) Kit decided to make an _____ pie for dinner. (wacky   apple)

   b) Carter's _____ were green with blue stripes. (pants   hands)

   c) Ravi _____ a mosquito on his arm. (scratched   smacked)

   d) Jill read the second book _____ reading the first book in

       the series. (always   after)

abacus	bamboo	cactus	discard	elasticity
forecast	graphic	hyena	Italy	lavender

1. Write the correct spelling word from the list to match the clue.

   a) A plant that packs its own needles _____

   b) The boot-shaped country that made pizza famous _____

   c) A plant with spikes of fragrant purple flowers _____

   d) A way to talk about how stretchy something is _____

   e) Another word for a drawing or an illustration _____

   f) A lightweight wood made from hollow plant stems _____

   g) Prediction of something in the future, such as weather _____

   h) Spotted dog-like animal that sounds like it's laughing _____

   i) Math device with beads that are slid along rows _____

   j) What happens to cards not used in a card game _____

2. Underline the words that have a short *a* sound.

   a) paste   slack   train   fast   calf   wears

   b) tackle   blanket   scrape   share   marry   habitat

   c) careful   laugh   blame   crayon   splash   crab

Say each word out loud. Listen for the short *e* sound.

Copy and spell each word three times using colours of your choice.

1. melody _____ _____ _____

2. pelican _____ _____ _____

3. Neptune _____ _____ _____

4. insect _____ _____ _____

5. level _____ _____ _____

6. ointment _____ _____ _____

7. active _____ _____ _____

8. kennel _____ _____ _____

9. pretzel _____ _____ _____

10. oxygen _____ _____ _____

Spelling Tip

The short *e* sound can be spelled with *ai* (*said*) or *ie* (*friend*).

Spelling Week 2 – Words with a Short *e* Sound

active	insect	kennel	level	melody
Neptune	ointment	oxygen	pelican	pretzel

1. Fill in the blank using the best spelling word from the list.

a) A _____ is a bird that scoops fish out of the water in its throat pouch.

b) The giant planet farthest from the Sun is called _____.

c) Mike's dog stays at the _____ when he has to go overseas.

d) The fairies played a strange sweet _____ with their tiny flutes.

e) A big green _____ landed on my arm just now! It surprised me!

f) My family goes for walks and bike rides to keep fit and _____.

g) The doctor gave us some _____ for the rash on my brother's leg.

h) Trees and plants take in carbon dioxide and produce _____.

i) My sister worked hard to get to the next _____ in karate class.

j) Our treat at the mall is a soft warm _____ with cheese dip.

Brain Stretch

How many spelling words can you fit into one sentence and still make sense? Give it a try!

1. Underline the words that have a short *e* sound.

   a) special   fleet   propel   gate   better   felt

   b) eyeball   lending   fresh   donkey   weather   spell

   c) grove   fender   squeak   lemming   reduce   wealth

   d) barrette   spread   seem   beach   elephant   teacher

   e) friend   cherry   sweep   kept   height   crest

2. Circle the word with the short *e* sound that makes the most sense.

   Write the word in the sentence.

   a) The _____ likes to live by the ocean where it can fish for food. (insect   pelican)

   b) We're going to the _____ to adopt a dog. (kennel   Neptune)

   c) The girl on stage played a beautiful _____ on the piano. (pretzel   melody)

   d) You should put some _____ on that insect bite. (ointment   oxygen)

3. The word *level* can have two meanings.

   Write a sentence to show each meaning of the word *level*.

   _____

   _____

active	insect	kennel	level	melody
Neptune	**ointment**	**oxygen**	**pelican**	**pretzel**

1. Write the correct spelling word from the list to match the clue.

a) Doing or ready to do physically energetic activities _____

b) A place where dogs or cats are boarded for a short time _____

c) A brittle or soft edible stick or knot sprinkled with salt _____

d) A pleasing string of musical notes _____

e) The giant planet farthest from the Sun; it has 14 moons _____

f) Flat and even; one stage of a game _____

g) A small animal with 6 legs, 3 body parts, at least
   2 wings, and a hard exoskeleton _____

h) An oil-based medicine applied to the skin _____

i) A colourless, odourless gas that is produced by plants
   and is necessary for all living things to breathe and live _____

j) A large ocean bird that has a throat pouch _____

2. Write a word that rhymes with the given word. The rhyming words do not have to be
   spelled in the same way.

a) shell _____   b) wealth _____   c) slept _____

Say each word out loud. Listen for the short *i* sound.

Copy and spell each word three times using colours of your choice.

1. hesitant   _____   _____   _____

2. jingle   _____   _____   _____

3. knitting   _____   _____   _____

4. comic   _____   _____   _____

5. asterisk   _____   _____   _____

6. millionth   _____   _____   _____

7. impossible   _____   _____   _____

8. distract   _____   _____   _____

9. picnic   _____   _____   _____

10. fantastic   _____   _____   _____

Brain Stretch

- Create a word search puzzle based on the spelling words.
- On a piece of paper, write a sentence using each spelling word.

Spelling Week 3 – Words with a Short *i* Sound

asterisk	comic	distract	fantastic	hesitant
impossible	jingle	knitting	millionth	picnic

1. Fill in the blank using the best spelling word from the list.

a) An _____ beside words usually means there's a note below.

b) Dee was _____ about joining the band, but she changed her mind.

c) One of my favourite hobbies is _____. I'm going to make a scarf!

d) Small bells inside the baby's rattle _____ when she shakes it.

e) Stan bought a new superhero _____ at the store today.

f) The department store had a big prize for their _____ customer.

g) To believe something is _____ is to make it so. Don't give up!

h) On Saturday, my whole family is going to the park for a _____.

i) Penny had to _____ the dog so Sam could grab his collar.

j) Watching the fireworks has always been a _____ experience.

Brain Stretch

How many spelling words can you fit into one sentence and still make sense?
Give it a try!

1. Circle the word with the short *i* sound that makes the most sense.

   Write the word in the sentence.

   a) Climbing to the top of this steep hill seems _____. (fantastic impossible)

   b) Maria is planning a nice _____ in the park tomorrow. (picnic comic)

   c) My mom and I take a _____ class every week. (business fitness)

2. Homophones are words that sound the same but are spelled differently.

   Write the homophone for the given word.

   a) billed _____   b) missed _____   c) witch _____

   d) gilt _____   e) links _____

3. How many syllables does the word have? Write the number beside the word.

   a) friendship _____   b) hippopotamus _____   c) dimly_____

4. Write a word that rhymes with the word below. The word does not have to be spelled the same to rhyme.

   a) milled _____   b) grit _____   c) gift _____

   d) mitten _____   e) flitter _____   f) slip _____

1. Use the word list below to look for the words in the puzzle.

   Circle the word in the word search puzzle. Then cross out the word in the list.

W	I	N	D	Y	C	R	I	B
R	F	K	D	L	M	S	T	I
I	R	I	E	C	C	W	R	T
D	F	T	Z	R	U	I	I	T
D	U	T	O	Z	P	S	M	E
E	Z	E	X	I	Y	N	E	N
N	S	N	N	D	I	I	R	E
N	Y	K	M	U	F	F	I	N
B	U	P	I	Y	L	F	F	J
L	D	R	I	P	X	U	T	Z

bitten	crib	drip	fizzy	kitten	muffin
ridden	rift	skip	sniff	trim	windy

2. Unscramble the spelling word. Write the correct spelling on the line.

a) tiktgnin _____

b) inpcic _____

c) crisdtta _____

d) lnjgie _____

e) hnlilmotio _____

f) stkreais _____

Say each word out loud. Listen for the short **o** sound.

Copy and spell each word three times using colours of your choice.

1. model _____ _____ _____

2. hospital _____ _____ _____

3. antibody _____ _____ _____

4. doctor _____ _____ _____

5. cousin _____ _____ _____

6. geometry _____ _____ _____

7. biology _____ _____ _____

8. dropped _____ _____ _____

9. flock _____ _____ _____

10. novel _____ _____ _____

Brain Stretch

- Create a word search puzzle based on the spelling words.
- On a piece of paper, write a sentence using each spelling word.

biology	cousin	doctor	dropped	fashion
flock	fond	hospital	model	novel

1. Fill in the blank using the best spelling word from the list.

a) My favourite _____ is Gulliver's Travels.

b) Rani is very _____ of helping her mom make homemade bread.

c) A huge _____ of Canada geese landed in the farmer's field.

d) Kevin likes the science of _____, which is about plants and animals.

e) My _____ Andrew is staying at our house all weekend.

f) The _____ said Kim had a bad cold and needed to stay in bed.

g) Ali accidentally _____ an egg on the floor and it smashed.

h) Our school had a _____ show to raise money for gym equipment.

i) Dad took us to the _____ to meet our new baby sister.

j) Kayla loves to put together _____ cars and airplanes.

Brain Stretch

How many spelling words can you fit into one sentence and still make sense?
Give it a try!

1. Circle the word with the short **o** sound that makes the most sense.

   Write the word in the sentence.

   a) Han wants to be a _____ when he grows up. (cousin   doctor)

   b) The birds gathered in a large _____ to fly south for the winter. (flock   pond)

   c) Tanya put together a dinosaur _____. (model   novel)

   d) The children are all very _____ of their math teacher. (sleepy   fond)

2. Write a word that rhymes with the given word. The rhyming word does not have to be spelled in the same way.

   a) dropped _____   b) flock _____   c) fond _____

   d) spot _____   e) boss _____   f) glove _____

   g) short _____   h) slop _____   i) long _____

3. Circle the words that have a short **o** sound.

   a) spool   glossy   flower   tonic   goalie   softly

   b) tropical   clown   cross   post   blond   shore

   c) snooze   pocket   strong   ghost   sparrow   fossil

biology	cousin	doctor	dropped	fashion
flock	fond	hospital	model	novel

1. Write the correct spelling word from the list to match the clue.

   a) A long fictional book that deals with human experiences _____

   b) The branch of science that deals with animals and
      plants and how they live   _____

   c) A small 3D representation of a much larger object   _____

   d) An institution that provides medical and surgical
      treatment and nursing care for sick and injured people _____

   e) A physician   _____

   f) Let or made something fall downward   _____

   g) Having an affection or liking for someone or something _____

   h) A large group of one type of bird, feeding, travelling,
      or resting together   _____

   i) A child of one's uncle or aunt   _____

   j) A popular trend in clothing styles   _____

2. Unscramble the spelling word. Write the correct spelling on the line.

a) ofnhias _____   b) dleom _____   c) scuoin _____

d) gbloiyo _____   e) codrot _____   f) ptshoali _____

Say each word out loud. Look at the different letters that make the short *u* sound.

Copy and spell each word three times using colours of your choice.

1. crumb

2. cluster

3. tumble

4. mustard

5. August

6. fungus

7. submarine

8. dull

9. bundle

10. volunteer

Spelling Tip

Words with *o* can have a short *u* sound (*Monday, month, mother*).

August   **bundle**   **cluster**   **crumb**   **dull**

fungus   **mustard**   **submarine**   **tumble**   **volunteer**

1. Fill in the blank using the best spelling word from the list.

a) The tiny mouse picked up a single _____ of the cookie.

b) Kenny says he wants to pilot a _____ some day.

c) The children love to _____ down the hill over and over again.

d) The tabletop is very _____ so Mom is rubbing polish on it.

e) Daisy wrapped all her toys in a blanket to make a _____ to carry.

f) Peter likes _____ on his hotdogs.

g) My family will _____ to help with the river cleanup next weekend.

h) A mushroom is a type of _____ that grows on rotting wood.

i) A large _____ of people formed around the cupcake table.

j) In _____, children start to get ready to go back to school.

Brain Stretch

How many spelling words can you fit into one sentence and still make sense?
Give it a try!

1. Circle the words that do **not** have a short **u** sound.

a) lunch   cloud   touch   rough   through

b) scuffle   button   bounce   rusty   cough

c) stuck   shout   flute   sponge   lunge

d) couch   bump   crumple   though   guest

2. Add a letter or letters to form a word with a short **u** sound. Write the word on the line.

a) _____ully   _____   b) _____ove   _____

c) _____uff   _____   d) _____uddle   _____

e) _____umble _____   f) _____ough   _____

3. Unscramble the spelling word. Write the correct spelling on the line.

a) dtsumra _____   b) olvretenu _____

c) lembtu _____   d) gfnusu _____

e) mcurb _____   f) gasutu _____

g) lsturce _____   h) niramsbeu _____

i) luld _____

Spelling Week 5 – Word Study

1. Use the word list below to look for the words in the puzzle.

   Circle the word in the word search puzzle. Then cross out the word in the list.

P	U	D	D	L	E	U	R	S
O	L	T	D	F	M	N	U	N
B	U	U	N	L	C	D	M	U
U	N	G	C	U	U	E	B	G
T	G	R	O	F	S	R	L	G
T	S	T	U	F	T	E	E	L
O	F	H	U	G	E	Z	H	E
N	F	L	U	M	B	E	R	H
C	U	S	T	A	R	D	B	J
D	R	T	T	L	T	U	G	Z

button	custard	fluff	hug	lumber	lungs
puddle	rumble	snuggle	tuft	tug	under

2. Write a word that rhymes with the word below. The word does not have to be spelled the same to rhyme.

   a) spun _____   b) rough _____   c) gummy _____

   d) crumble _____   e) blunder _____   f) grumpy _____

Say each word out loud. Listen for the long *a* sound.

Copy and spell each word three times using colours of your choice.

1. canine _____ _____ _____

2. daisy _____ _____ _____

3. afraid _____ _____ _____

4. greatest _____ _____ _____

5. complain _____ _____ _____

6. hurricane _____ _____ _____

7. container _____ _____ _____

8. ancient _____ _____ _____

9. indicate _____ _____ _____

10. arrange _____ _____ _____

Spelling Tips: The long *a* sound can be spelled with

- letters *ai* (*quail*)
- letter *a* followed by a **consonant + e** (*earthquake*)
- letters *ay* (*relay*)

afraid	ancient	arrange	canine	complain
container	daisy	greatest	hurricane	indicate

1. Fill in the blank using the best spelling word from the list.

a) I take my lunch to school in a reusable _____ .

b) My grandfather grew the largest pink _____ I've ever seen.

c) The town had to board up their windows to prepare for the _____.

d) Doing well at public speaking is Frank's _____ accomplishment.

e) The dark clouds approaching _____ that a storm is coming.

f) I used to be _____ of thunderstorms, but now I enjoy watching them.

g) Maddy likes to _____ her marbles in groups by colour and pattern.

h) Your _____ teeth are the slightly pointy ones in the top teeth.

i) Our cat likes to _____ when her food dish is empty.

j) Gladiators fought in the Colosseum in _____ Rome.

Brain Stretch

How many spelling words can you fit into one sentence and still make sense? Give it a try!

1. Say the word out loud. Underline the words with the long *a* sound.

a) state	meal	rake	scale	peach
b) shake	tall	crazy	soap	grate
c) paste	lean	train	unreal	clay
d) parade	spark	quake	cheat	sway

2. Look around the room. See the objects and say their names out loud. Write down as many objects as you can find that have a long *a* sound.

_____

_____

_____

_____

3. Write a short story using as many of the words as you can from Question 2.

_____

_____

_____

_____

1. Use the word list below to look for the words in the puzzle.

   Circle the word in the word search puzzle. Then cross out the word in the list.

S	P	E	A	K	B	C	L	W
G	R	A	T	E	L	E	A	A
Y	A	L	A	Z	Y	O	P	V
B	C	X	C	A	I	I	A	Y
E	H	W	I	T	S	S	R	L
A	E	T	R	A	I	N	A	G
R	Q	Y	M	M	G	D	D	E
C	R	A	T	E	R	L	E	H
I	E	M	A	I	L	M	B	J
D	R	X	R	A	Y	U	G	Z

ache	**bear**	**crater**	**email**	**grate**	**lazy**
parade	**speak**	**tame**	**train**	**wavy**	**xray**

2. Write a word that rhymes with the word below. The word does not have to be spelled the same to rhyme.

   a) pair _____   b) shake _____   c) flame _____

   d) waste _____   e) clay _____   f) stain _____

Say each word out loud. Look at the different letters that make the long *e* sound.

Copy and spell each word three times using colours of your choice.

1. beetle   _____ _____ _____

2. eager   _____ _____ _____

3. adhere   _____ _____ _____

4. increase   _____ _____ _____

5. breathe   _____ _____ _____

6. museum   _____ _____ _____

7. chief   _____ _____ _____

8. eagle   _____ _____ _____

9. reason   _____ _____ _____

10. appeal   _____ _____ _____

Spelling Tips: The long *e* sound can be spelled with

- letter *e* by itself, and *e* followed by a **consonant + e** (*detail, evening*)
- letters **ee**, **ea**, and **ie** (*steel, teach, field*)
- letters **y** and **ey** (*guppy, monkey*)

Spelling Week 7 – Words with a Long *e* Sound

adhere	appeal	beetle	breathe	chief
eager	eagle	increase	museum	reason

1. Fill in the blank using the best spelling word from the list.

a) Some people believe that everything in life happens for a _____.

b) Dan is _____ to show his friends the new magic trick he learned.

c) My favourite part of the _____ is the dinosaur exhibit.

d) Walking out in the forest, Liz feels she can finally _____ and relax.

e) If the batter is too dry, we will have to _____ the amount of liquid.

f) A shiny green _____ landed on a plant near me.

g) A beautiful bald _____ was fishing in the river in British Columbia.

h) The fire _____ received an award for 25 years of service.

i) The smell of the freshly baked pizza had a strong _____ for Jack.

j) Kim forgot the water, so the wallpaper wouldn't _____ to the wall.

Brain Stretch

How many spelling words can you fit into one sentence and still make sense? Give it a try!

1. Unscramble the spelling word. Write the correct spelling on the line.

a) sumume _____   b) geera _____   c) edearh _____

d) plapae _____   e) aiscnree _____   f) hfeic _____

g) serona _____   h) tbrehea _____   i) geela _____

2. Circle the words that have a long **e** sound.

a)	shield	mean	rest	ever	donkey
b)	shell	belief	even	greet	guest
c)	tweek	bunny	clever	treat	festival
d)	prey	steak	creek	valley	quest
e)	speak	never	meek	fairy	skeleton

3. Compound words are two smaller words put together to make one bigger word.
   Draw a line between the two smaller words in the bigger word.

a)	cartwheel	monkey	blueberry	bicycle	earthquake
b)	seastar	butter	about	fireworks	headband
c)	shadow	earlobe	binder	fingernail	stingray
d)	nosebleed	thunder	eyelash	ponytail	berries

adhere	appeal	beetle	breathe	chief
eager	eagle	increase	museum	reason

1. Write the correct spelling word from the list to match the clue.

a) A leader or ruler of a people or clan _____

b) Large bird of prey _____

c) An insect that has hard wing coverings _____

d) To make or become greater in size, amount, etc. _____

e) Cause, justification, or explanation for an action or event _____

f) Wanting to do or have something very much _____

g) To take air into the lungs, then expel it _____

h) To stick firmly to something _____

i) Be attractive or interesting _____

j) A building in which objects of historical, scientific, artistic, or cultural interest are stored and exhibited _____

2. Do **not** use the spelling word list for this activity. Write 2 words that have a long **e** sound made by the following letters:

a) ee _____ b) ie _____

c) y _____ d) ea _____

Say each word out loud. Listen for the long *i* sound.

Copy and spell each word three times using colours of your choice.

1. define _____ _____ _____

2. combine _____ _____ _____

3. assign _____ _____ _____

4. entire _____ _____ _____

5. cacti _____ _____ _____

6. feline _____ _____ _____

7. graphite _____ _____ _____

8. climb _____ _____ _____

9. delight _____ _____ _____

10. dried _____ _____ _____

Spelling Tips: The long *i* sound can be spelled with

- letters *igh* and *ign* (*frighten, sighed*)
- letter *i* followed by **consonant + e** (*while*)
- letters *ie* and *y* (*pie, shy*)

Spelling Week 8 – Words with a Long *i* Sound

assign	cacti	climb	combine	define
delight	dried	entire	feline	graphite

1. Fill in the blank using the best spelling word from the list.

a) Cats are members of the _____ family.

b) My aunt has a large collection of different _____ in cute planters.

c) The teacher asked us to _____ the word "ambition."

d) In just a few minutes, our dog ate the _____ pizza.

e) Pencil leads are made from a soft, grey material called _____.

f) Grandpa collected flowers and _____ them for Grandma to keep.

g) Imagine her _____ when she opened the box and saw a puppy!

h) My friends and I decided to _____ to the very top of big hill.

i) The recipe says to carefully _____ the ingredients in a large bowl.

j) Every Friday, our French teacher likes to _____ homework.

Brain Stretch

How many spelling words can you fit into one sentence and still make sense? Give it a try!

1. Say the word out loud. Underline the words with the long *i* sound.

   a) twine   cringe   sigh   skinny   lightning

   b) shipping   flight   lazy   smile   cry

   c) field   sign   print   rhyme   write

   d) grime   cycle   sick   white   marry

   e) spice   citizen   flair   dried   hire

2. A **synonym** is a word that means the same as another word.

   Circle the synonym for the bolded word.

   a) **spine**   elbow   backbone   b) **shy**   timid   bold

3. Circle the word with the long *i* sound that makes the most sense.

   Write the word in the sentence.

   a) Mom planted some new _____ today. (cacti   felines)

   b) Milk is _____ with flour, eggs, and sugar to make batter. (dried   combined)

   c) Our teacher _____ the space project to me and Mitch. (defined   assigned)

   d) If you don't catch that spider now, it will _____ too high to reach. (smile   climb)

   e) We need to _____ the board with the brush to clean it. (climb   wipe)

Spelling Week 8 – Word Study

1. Use the word list below to look for the words in the puzzle.

   Circle the word in the word search puzzle. Then cross out the word in the list.

S	P	R	I	T	E	T	K	W
G	R	I	N	D	L	I	N	H
Y	R	K	A	Z	Y	L	I	Y
C	C	I	C	A	I	E	F	Y
Y	H	I	M	T	S	S	E	F
C	Y	F	R	E	I	N	A	L
L	E	R	M	M	G	D	D	I
E	N	Y	T	E	R	L	E	G
I	A	L	I	G	N	M	B	H
H	E	I	G	H	T	U	G	T

align   **cycle**   **flight**   **fry**   **grime**   **grind**

height   **hyena**   **knife**   **sprite**   **tile**   **why**

2. Write a word that rhymes with the word below. The word does not have to be spelled the same to rhyme.

   a) shine _____   b) spike _____   c) rye _____

   d) style _____   e) height _____   f) slide _____

Spelling Week 9 – Words with a Long *o* Sound

Say each word out loud. Look at the different letters that make the long *o* sound.

Copy and spell each word three times using colours of your choice.

1. gopher _____ _____ _____

2. frozen _____ _____ _____

3. radio _____ _____ _____

4. polar _____ _____ _____

5. ocean _____ _____ _____

6. locate _____ _____ _____

7. Mexico _____ _____ _____

8. calico _____ _____ _____

9. golden _____ _____ _____

10. motion _____ _____ _____

Spelling Tips: A long *o* sound can be made with

- letter *o* (*troll, bonus, so*)
- letters *oe* (*doe*)
- letters *oa* and *ow* (*foal, throw*)
- letter *o* followed by a *consonant + e* (*pole*)

Spelling Week 9 – Words with a Long *o* Sound

calico	frozen	golden	gopher	locate
Mexico	motion	ocean	polar	radio

1. Fill in the blank using the best spelling word from the list.

   a) A raccoon walked by and our _____ detector turned on.

   b) The _____ is mostly unexplored and mysterious.

   c) Antarctica's land mass is _____ all year round.

   d) Our cat is orange, black, and white. She is a _____ cat.

   e) One of my favourite stories is about a princess with a _____ ball.

   f) Mr. Smith will be travelling to _____ on his next vacation.

   g) Aunt Jill loves to listen to old songs on the _____.

   h) A _____ is often thought to be a groundhog, but it's a different animal.

   i) Ken used a map to _____ South America and Peru.

   j) In the winter, _____ bears hunt on the ice sheets in the Arctic.

Brain Stretch

How many spelling words can you fit into one sentence and still make sense? Give it a try!

1. Underline the words in the story that have a long **o** sound.

A long time ago, there was a mean lion who was king of the jungle. One day, a little mouse ran across the lion's paw when he was sleeping and the lion woke up. He caught the mouse by the tail. "Please let me go!" cried the mouse. The lion said, "Why should I let you go?" The mouse said, "If you let me go, one day I may be able to help you." The lion laughed. "How could a tiny mouse like you ever help a big lion like me?" he said. "Although I am small," said the mouse, "I just might surprise you." The lion thought it was so funny that he let the mouse go free. The mouse thanked him and ran off.

One day, some men came into the jungle and captured the lion in a big net. The lion roared in fear, but there was no way he could get out. The men left the lion tied to a tree while they hunted for more animals to capture. The little mouse heard the lion roaring and ran to him. The tiny mouse used his teeth to gnaw a hole in the net large enough for the lion to escape. The lion thanked the mouse and ran off. From that day forward, the lion no longer judged an animal solely by its size.

2. An **antonym** is a word that has the opposite meaning of another word.

Circle the antonym for the bolded word.

a) **locate**   find   miss

b) **frozen**   thawed   solid

3. What does **flowed** mean in the sentence? Circle the correct definition.

Amy's red hair flowed over her shoulders.

moved at a steady pace   hung loosely and gracefully

calico	frozen	golden	gopher	locate
Mexico	motion	ocean	polar	radio

1. Write the correct spelling word from the list to match the clue.

   a) A small burrowing rodent with cheek pouches   _____

   b) A black, orange, and white pattern on a female cat   _____

   c) The whole body of salt water that covers nearly

   three-quarters of Earth's surface   _____

   d) Movement   _____

   e) Made of, the colour of, or shining like gold   _____

   f) Having to do with the Arctic or Antarctic region   _____

   g) The country right below the United States   _____

   h) Find the exact position of a place or thing   _____

   i) Turned into ice by extreme cold   _____

   j) A device that transmits and receives electromagnetic

   waves that carry sound messages   _____

2. Do **not** use the spelling word list for this activity. Write 2 words that have the long *o*

   sound made by the following letters:

   a) oe _____   b) oa _____

   c) ow _____   d) o _____

Say each word out loud. Look at the different letters that make the long *u* sound.

Copy and spell each word three times using colours of your choice.

1. cashew _____ _____ _____

2. genuine _____ _____ _____

3. graduate _____ _____ _____

4. tissue _____ _____ _____

5. rescue _____ _____ _____

6. uniform _____ _____ _____

7. annual _____ _____ _____

8. casual _____ _____ _____

9. jewel _____ _____ _____

10. feud _____ _____ _____

Spelling Tips: A long *u* sound can be made with

- letter *u* followed by a **consonant + e** (*reuse*)
- letter *u* followed by a **consonant + i** or *y* (*cupid, jury*)
- letters *ue* (*cue*)
- letters *ew* (*few, ewe*)

Spelling Week 10 – Words with a Long *u* Sound

annual	cashew	casual	feud	genuine
graduate	jewel	rescue	tissue	uniform

1. Fill in the blank using the best spelling word from the list.

a) On _____ Fridays, my parents get to wear jeans to work.

b) Every October, we have our _____ bake sale at school.

c) Dad placed a perfect _____ on top of each cupcake.

d) My cousin Jeff works as an animal _____ officer.

e) The ring contained a very large blue _____.

f) Lisa was sneezing a lot, so she needed a _____.

g) This Friday, we will all _____ from Grade 5.

h) Aunt Jo works for the police, so she wears a blue _____.

i) The neighbours across the road have had a _____ going for years.

j) Some people feel they have to be fake, but it's best to be _____.

Brain Stretch

How many spelling words can you fit into one sentence and still make sense? Give it a try!

Long vowels say their name! So when you say words with long vowels, you hear the letter names **A** (game), **E** (team), **I** (bite), **O** (goat), and **U** (use).

The long **u** should sound just like the word **you**. For example, the word **June** sounds like **Jyoune**. Other letter combinations, such as **ew**, **ue**, and a **consonant + e**, **i**, or **y**, can also make the long **u** sound. However, all of those letters, including **u** itself, can also make other sounds that do not sound like the word **you**.

1. Say the word out loud. Listen for sounds the letters make. Underline the words that have the long **u** sound.

a) rescue	cue	clue	flu	unite
b) true	university	grew	menu	yule
c) chew	music	argue	flew	true
d) rescue	view	blue	unique	grew

2. The word **pupil** can have two meanings.

   Write a sentence to show each meaning of the word **pupil**.

   _____

   _____

3. Write a sentence using the word **communicate**.

   _____

1. Use the word list below to look for the words in the puzzle.

   Circle the word in the word search puzzle. Then cross out the word in the list.

U	N	I	C	Y	C	L	E	A
N	E	I	D	L	M	N	O	R
I	R	C	E	C	O	O	Z	G
Q	C	C	U	E	I	C	Y	U
U	X	W	U	U	E	L	J	E
E	U	I	E	P	T	Z	E	G
V	N	D	W	F	I	E	W	E
O	I	Y	E	W	T	D	E	H
I	T	R	E	U	S	E	L	J
R	E	S	C	U	E	U	G	Z

argue	cue	cupid	ewe	jewel	June
rescue	reuse	unicycle	unique	unite	yew

2. Just for fun, let's look at some other letter combinations and words that have a long **u** sound. The letter combinations include **oo**, **oe**, **ui**, and **ugh**. Say the words out loud. Use the pronunciation key to pronounce any words you don't know.

shoo and shoe [shyou]   manual [man-you-ull]   Hugh [hyou]

juice [jyouss]   ukulele [you-kuh-lay-lee]   ewe [you]

Say each word out loud. Listen for the long **i** and long **e** sounds.

Copy and spell each word three times using colours of your choice.

1. balcony _____ _____ _____

2. hydrogen_____ _____ _____

3. archery _____ _____ _____

4. identify _____ _____ _____

5. delivery _____ _____ _____

6. apology _____ _____ _____

7. cyclone _____ _____ _____

8. kayak _____ _____ _____

9. hydrate _____ _____ _____

10. colony _____ _____ _____

Brain Stretch

- Create a word search puzzle based on the spelling words.
- On a piece of paper, write a sentence using each spelling word.

apology	archery	balcony	colony	cyclone
delivery	hydrate	hydrogen	identify	kayak

1. Fill in the blank using the best spelling word from the list.

a) I get very nervous when I go near the edge of my uncle's _____.

b) I'm learning to use a bow and arrow in _____ class.

c) My friend said something mean to me. Later he gave me an _____.

d) One oxygen molecule and two _____ molecules make water.

e) I'm using a bird handbook so I can learn to _____ the birds I see.

f) Sam took the _____ out on the choppy water. It was fun!

g) Make sure you _____ on hot days by drinking lots of water.

h) Tonight, we are waiting for the pizza _____ man.

i) There is a huge ant _____ under the bush in our backyard.

j) The weather report warned of a dangerous _____ approaching.

Brain Stretch

How many spelling words can you fit into one sentence and still make sense? Give it a try!

1. Read the sentence clue. Unscramble the word and write it in the space.

   a) A _____ is another word for a hurricane. (lnceyco)

   b) I'm learning how to roll over and roll back up in a _____. (yaakk)

   c) Dave is becoming very accurate with a bow in _____. (cerahyr)

   d) The investigator worked hard to _____ the criminal. (dfytieni)

   e) We can order food to pick up or we can get _____. (vdliyere)

   f) There is a beautiful view when you step out onto the _____. (cybnalo)

2. Circle the compound words. Write the two words that make the word with a **+** sign.

   Example: *doghouse*   *dog + house*

   a) bookshelf   deny   fly   daydream   crayon

   _____

   b) cherry   someone   monkey   apply   bodyguard

   _____

   c) delay   strawberry   berry   firefighter   afraid

   _____

| apology | archery | balcony | colony | cyclone |
| delivery | hydrate | hydrogen | identify | kayak |

1. Write the correct spelling word from the list to match the clue.

a) A community of one kind of animal or plant living
   close together   _____

b) To take in or absorb water   _____

c) The practice of shooting with a bow and arrow   _____

d) A system of winds that rotate around a strong centre
   of low atmospheric pressure   _____

e) Expression of regret for something done or said   _____

f) The action of delivering something, such as goods   _____

g) To find out or show who someone or what something is   _____

h) A platform enclosed by a wall or railing on the outside
   of a building   _____

i) A colourless, odourless, highly flammable gas   _____

j) A light, narrow boat with pointed ends and a hole in
   the top to sit in   _____

2. The word *type* can have two meanings. Write a sentence to show each meaning.

_____

_____

Say each word out loud. Think about what letter or letters are missing.

Copy and spell each word three times using colours of your choice.

1. it's _____ _____ _____

2. he'll _____ _____ _____

3. you're _____ _____ _____

4. couldn't _____ _____ _____

5. I've _____ _____ _____

6. they'll _____ _____ _____

7. haven't _____ _____ _____

8. we've _____ _____ _____

9. won't _____ _____ _____

10. she'd _____ _____ _____

Brain Stretch

- Create a word search puzzle based on the spelling words.
- On a piece of paper, write a sentence using each spelling word.

Spelling Week 12 – Contractions

couldn't	haven't	he'll	it's	I've
she'd	they'll	we've	won't	you're

1. Fill in the blank using the best spelling word from the list.

a) I heard that _____ having a special cake for your birthday.

b) Trish's baby sister _____ stand by herself when I last saw her.

c) I told my mom _____ decided to play the flute in music class.

d) You will need a jacket because _____ chilly outside today.

e) Jimmy said he _____ ever go near that big spider.

f) _____ be happy to find out he's getting an award in spelling.

g) Kelly said _____ bought the wrong kind of flour.

h) I have to paint a picture, but I _____ got a good idea yet.

i) _____ all decided to have our lunch in the park today.

j) Max and Milly said _____ be going on vacation to Alberta in June.

Brain Stretch

How many spelling words can you fit into one sentence and still make sense? Give it a try!

There are two tricky contractions. You will have to learn these contractions.

will not = won't   **cannot = can't**

1. Circle the incorrect contraction.

   Write the correct contraction at the end of the sentence.

   a)   David willn't be coming to my party this weekend. _____

   b)   I cann't wait for summer holidays to get here! _____

   c)   Sara wil'nt tell May's secret to anyone. _____

   d)   Jon cant see clearly without his glasses. _____

   e)   Donot you want to swim with us tomorrow? _____

   f)   Hasnot she seen this movie before? _____

2. Read the contraction. Write the words in full.

   Example: I'm   I am

   a) couldn't _____   b) hasn't _____

   c) we're _____   d) she'd _____

   e) that's _____   f) don't _____

   g) can't _____   h) won't _____

   i) you'll _____   j) he's _____

1. You are going to decode a secret message! The letters of the alphabet are each represented by a number, as shown below.

1	2	3	4	5	6	7	8	9	10	11	12	13
A	B	C	D	E	F	G	H	I	J	K	L	M

14	15	16	17	18	19	20	21	22	23	24	25	26
N	O	P	Q	R	S	T	U	V	W	X	Y	Z

Write the letter on the line above the number to decode the message.

a) _____ ' __ / _____ / _____ / _____ / _____

   9 20 19   14 15 20   23 8 1 20   25 15 21   12 15 15 11

_____ / _____ / _____ , / _____

 1 20   20 8 1 20   13 1 20 20 5 18 19   9 20 19

_____ / _____ / _____ .

 23 8 1 20   25 15 21   19 5 5

b) _____ ' / ____ / _____ / _____ / __

 9 19 14 20   9 20   1 13 1 26 9 14 7   8 15 23   1

_____ / _____ / _____ / _____ / __

 16 5 18 19 15 14   23 8 15   23 1 19   15 14 3 5   1

_____ / _____ / _____

 19 20 18 1 14 7 5 18   3 1 14   19 21 4 4 5 14 12 25

_____ / _____ / _____ / _____ ?

 2 5 3 15 13 5   25 15 21 18   2 5 19 20   6 18 9 5 14 4

Say each word out loud. Watch for the double consonants.

Copy and spell each word three times using colours of your choice.

1. collect   _____   _____   _____

2. fizz   _____   _____   _____

3. babble   _____   _____   _____

4. annoying _____   _____   _____

5. fluff   _____   _____   _____

6. carried   _____   _____   _____

7. arrange   _____   _____   _____

8. shell   _____   _____   _____

9. grass   _____   _____   _____

10. batter   _____   _____   _____

Brain Stretch

- Create a word search puzzle based on the spelling words.
- On a piece of paper, write a sentence using each spelling word.

Spelling Week 13 – Double Consonants

annoying	arrange	babble	batter	carried
collect	fizz	fluff	grass	shell

1. Fill in the blank using the best spelling word from the list.

a) The mother fox _____ her kits one by one into a hole in the ground.

b) My sister Anna likes to _____ all her toys according to their size.

c) Ken and Kathy are making the _____ for blueberry pancakes.

d) Our dog Buster is _____ Mrs. Grady's cat again.

e) I like to _____ pretty stones and shells at the beach.

f) My baby cousin Danny is just starting to _____.

g) When you pour pop into a glass, it starts to _____ and foams up.

h) When I hold the big _____ up to my ear, I can hear the sea.

i) In spring, our poplar trees have catkins covered in white _____.

j) Clovers and tiny violets grow in the _____ in our backyard.

Brain Stretch

How many spelling words can you fit into one sentence and still make sense? Give it a try!

For many verbs that end with **consonant + vowel + consonant**, double the final consonant before adding **ed** or **ing**.

Examples:	Verb	Add ed	Add ing
	fan	fanned	fanning
	snap	snapped	snapping

1. Add **ed** and **ing** to the verb. Remember to double the final consonant when needed.

a) grab _____ _____

b) knit _____ _____

c) cross _____ _____

d) plant _____ _____

e) prefer _____ _____

2. Put a ✔ beside the word if it is spelled correctly. If the word is spelled incorrectly, put an **X** beside the word and write the word correctly.

a) showwing _____   b) painted _____

c) slipped _____   d) washhing _____

e) traveled _____   f) meltting _____

g) coughed _____   h) walkking _____

1. Use the word list below to look for the words in the puzzle.

   Circle the word in the word search puzzle. Then cross out the word in the list.

B	U	G	G	E	D	E	G	S
B	A	L	L	O	O	N	U	C
C	O	M	M	O	N	A	P	R
U	Z	P	I	Z	Z	A	P	I
D	I	N	N	E	R	A	Y	B
D	P	F	Y	S	T	E	D	B
L	P	D	O	L	L	A	R	L
E	E	Z	B	T	U	Z	E	E
S	R	A	C	C	O	O	N	R
C	H	A	L	L	E	N	G	E

balloon   **bugged**   **challenge**   **common**   **cuddle**   **dinner**

dollar   **guppy**   **pizza**   **raccoon**   **scribble**   **zipper**

2. Write a word that rhymes with the word below. The words do not have to be spelled the same.

a) fall _____   b) fitter _____   c) mill _____

d) clatter _____   e) toss _____   f) penny _____

g) bunny _____   h) tell _____   i) hill _____

Say each word out loud. Listen for which letters you don't hear.

Copy and spell each word three times using colours of your choice.

1. bruise _____ _____ _____

2. drizzle _____ _____ _____

3. caught _____ _____ _____

4. honest _____ _____ _____

5. escape _____ _____ _____

6. salmon _____ _____ _____

7. crumb _____ _____ _____

8. glisten _____ _____ _____

9. design _____ _____ _____

10. knead _____ _____ _____

Spelling Tip

For many words that end in a vowel followed by a
consonant + silent e, the **e** makes the vowel say its name.

Spelling Week 14 – Words with Silent Letters

bruise	caught	crumb	design	drizzle
escape	glisten	honest	knead	salmon

1. Fill in the blank using the best spelling word from the list.

a) The last step in making this cake is to _____ thin icing over the top.

b) Wally bought a fish tank for his mouse so it wouldn't _____.

c) I have a big _____ on my leg, but I don't know where it came from.

d) Our science project is to _____ and build a working volcano.

e) Peter _____ a leopard frog at the pond this afternoon.

f) When our dog Lexie eats, she doesn't leave even one _____.

g) In the morning sun, spider webs _____ with drops of dew.

h) A good habit to have is to always be _____ with people.

i) In British Columbia, bears have a feast when the _____ migrate.

j) Dad has me help him _____ the bread so it will rise properly.

Brain Stretch

How many spelling words can you fit into one sentence and still make sense?
Give it a try!

1. Say the word out loud. Can you hear all the letter sounds? Circle words with silent letters. Underline the silent letters.

a) through   tube   scoop   flu   honest

b) muscle   unique   yellow   menu   fuse

c) school   lump   argue   crew   talk

d) books   view   true   knight   listen

e) calf   wag   thumb   shook   gnome

2. Say the word out loud. Add **e** to the end of the word. Write the new word. Say the word again. Even though the **e** is silent, it still changes the way the vowel sounds.

	Add e		Add e
a) far		b) twin	
c) shin		d) cut	
e) star		f) scrap	
g) fad		h) dim	

3. What happens to the vowel when you add **e** to the end of the word?

_____

4. Say the word out loud. Write **L** if the vowel has a long sound or **S** if it has a short sound.

a) spare ___   b) litter ___   c) flight ___   d) plain ___

e) fraction ___   f) tray ___   g) funny ___   h) male ___

| bruise | caught | crumb | design | drizzle |
| escape | glisten | honest | knead | salmon |

1. Write the correct spelling word from the list to match the clue.

   a) To work something with the hands to form a dough   _____

   b) A large edible fish with reddish or pinkish flesh   _____

   c) A plan or drawing to show the function and look of

   something before it is built or made   _____

   d) Captured   _____

   e) To shine or glitter   _____

   f) A discolouration of the skin in an area of injury   _____

   g) A light rain falling in very fine drops; to trickle a liquid,

   such as oil, melted butter, or thin icing, over food   _____

   h) A very small fragment of something   _____

   i) To break free from confinement or control   _____

   j) Sincere and truthful   _____

2. Do **not** use the spelling word list for this activity. Write a word that has the following

   silent letters:

   a) wr _____   b) gh _____

   c) b _____   d) t _____

Say each word out loud. Look at the different letters that make the long and short *oo* sounds.
Copy and spell each word three times using colours of your choice.

1. crooked _____ _____ _____

2. stood _____ _____ _____

3. aloof _____ _____ _____

4. loom _____ _____ _____

5. mistook _____ _____ _____

6. grew _____ _____ _____

7. brook _____ _____ _____

8. tomb _____ _____ _____

9. bamboo _____ _____ _____

10. would _____ _____ _____

Spelling Tips

The long *oo* sound can be spelled with
- letters **ew** (*flew*) and **ue** (*glue*)
- letters **oo** (*moon*)
- letters **ough** (*through*)

The short *oo* sound can be spelled with
- letters **oo** (*book*)
- letters **ou** (*could*)

brook	cartoon	hood	noodle	rooster
scoop	shook	smoothie	stood	wool

1. Fill in the blank using the best spelling word from the list.

a) My brother uses his toy truck to _____ dirt and dump it out again.

b) On my grandparents' farm, Rocky the _____ crows every morning.

c) Tiny silver minnows swim in the little _____ in the forest.

d) Aunt Hazel's sheep produce very good _____ to make yarn.

e) The earthquake _____ the books off the shelf at our house.

f) We watched a _____ called *Betty Boop* from my grandmother's time.

g) My sister plays jokes on me by putting things in my _____.

h) Mom made a mixed berry _____ to share with me for breakfast.

i) I accidentally dropped a _____ on the floor and our dog ate it.

j) Dad and I _____ by the window to watch the big thunderstorm.

Brain Stretch

How many spelling words can you fit into one sentence and still make sense? Give it a try!

1. Circle the words that have a long **oo** sound. Some of the words have the same sound but are spelled differently.

   a) wood   tuna   tough   grew   glue

   b) true   drew   shoulder   cloud   fruit

   c) loop   grumpy   goose   hours   clue

   d) hooks   preview   soup   gloomy   enough

2. Circle the words that have a short **oo** sound. Some of the words have the same sound but are spelled differently.

   a) stood   gold   would   flu   took

   b) mole   wood   threw   could   woof

   c) crook   caboose   nook   blew   bull

   d) foot   view   cookie   brook   soot

3. Write the correct letter beside the word. Write **S** for a short **oo** sound, **L** for a long **oo** sound, and **N** for neither sound.

   a) cook _____   b) cuff _____   c) spoon _____

   d) fool _____   e) frown _____   f) should _____

   g) tongue _____   h) shook _____   i) blue _____

1. Use the word list below to look for the words in the puzzle.

   Circle the word in the word search puzzle. Then cross out the word in the list.

T	C	R	U	E	L	J	B	K
F	O	O	T	P	R	I	N	T
B	O	G	S	R	W	G	S	X
O	K	H	H	F	I	O	P	B
O	I	O	O	D	V	O	O	R
K	E	U	O	S	T	D	O	O
L	R	L	K	O	T	B	L	O
E	W	O	U	L	D	Y	I	M
T	O	O	L	S	D	E	B	J
B	P	Y	W	L	O	O	T	Z

booklet	broom	cookie	cruel	footprint	ghoul
goodbye	loot	spool	tools	shook	would

2. Write a word that rhymes with the word below. Rhyming words do not have to be

   spelled in the same way.

   a) flute _____

   b) crook _____

   c) croon _____

   d) doom _____

   e) pull _____

   f) brew _____

   g) cruel _____

   h) should _____

   i) loose _____

Say each word out loud. Listen to the sounds *oi* and *oy* make.

Copy and spell each word three times using colours of your choice.

1. destroy _____ _____ _____

2. enjoy _____ _____ _____

3. avoid _____ _____ _____

4. poison _____ _____ _____

5. oyster _____ _____ _____

6. asteroid _____ _____ _____

7. choice _____ _____ _____

8. moisture _____ _____ _____

9. voyage _____ _____ _____

10. noisy _____ _____ _____

Brain Stretch

- Create a word search puzzle based on the spelling words.
- On a piece of paper, write a sentence using each spelling word.

asteroid	avoid	choice	destroy	enjoy
loyal	moisture	noisy	oyster	voyage

1. Fill in the blank using the best spelling word from the list.

a) Our neighbour has a pet rooster that is very _____ in the mornings.

b) The _____ belt is a region between the orbits of Jupiter and Mars.

c) Our grandma gave us the _____ of baking cookies or cupcakes.

d) My pet rat Winston likes to _____ all of his blankets and toys.

e) Captain Cook went on a _____ from England to North America.

f) My aunt's dog Taffy is a very _____ companion for her.

g) When Dad takes a shower, _____ collects on the bathroom mirror.

h) I try to _____ the corner house because their dog barks at me.

i) When a little sand gets into an _____, it forms a pearl.

j) I really _____ singing and dancing to my favourite songs.

Brain Stretch

How many spelling words can you fit into one sentence and still make sense? Give it a try!

1. Read the sentence clue. Unscramble the spelling word and write it in the space.

   a) When my best friend Karen is mad at me, she tries hard to _____ me. (dovia)

   b) We must not be _____ when someone is sleeping. (soniy)

   c) Treat your pets with kindness and they'll become _____ friends. (yloal)

   d) When given the _____, I would rather participate than observe. (ohicec)

   e) Tent caterpillars will _____ all the leaves on a tree branch. (odteyrs)

   f) We're going on a long ocean _____ next month. (yvgaeo)

2. Circle the compound words. Write the two words that make the word with a **+** sign.

   Example: *brainstorm   brain + storm*

   a) boardwalk   rely   kitten   earthworm   dragon

      _____

   b) berries   downpour   donkey   footprint   cheesecake

      _____

   c) grapevine   fireplace   merry   cornstalk   elephant

      _____

asteroid	avoid	choice	destroy	enjoy
loyal	moisture	noisy	oyster	voyage

1. Write the correct spelling word from the list to match the clue.

   a) To take delight or pleasure in something _____

   b) A mollusc that has a rough shell and can produce pearls _____

   c) A small rocky body that orbits the Sun _____

   d) Making a lot of loud or unpleasant noise _____

   e) To keep away from or stop oneself from doing something _____

   f) A long journey by sea or in space _____

   g) The act of selecting or make a decision when faced
      with two or more possibilities _____

   h) To put an end to the existence of something _____

   i) Able to give or show firm and constant support _____

   j) Water or other liquid spread as a vapour, within a solid,
      or condensed on a surface _____

2. Do **not** use the spelling word list for this activity. Write four words that contain the
   following letters:

   a) oi _____

   b) oy _____

Say each word out loud. Listen for the *ow* sound.

Copy and spell each word three times using colours of your choice.

1. compound   _____   _____   _____

2. browse   _____   _____   _____

3. powerful   _____   _____   _____

4. announcer   _____   _____   _____

5. coward   _____   _____   _____

6. allow   _____   _____   _____

7. cloudy   _____   _____   _____

8. downtown   _____   _____   _____

9. pouch   _____   _____   _____

10. outside   _____   _____   _____

Brain Stretch

- Create a word search puzzle based on the spelling words.
- On a piece of paper, write a sentence using each spelling word.

allow	announcer	browse	cloudy	compound
coward	downtown	outside	pouch	powerful

1. Fill in the blank using the best spelling word from the list.

a) For a fun day in the summertime, my family goes walking _____.

b) In winter, our dog Trixie loves to play _____ in the snow.

c) If I finish my homework, Mom will _____ me to play video games.

d) I was hoping for sunshine today, but the sky is all _____ instead.

e) The _____ called the name of the lucky person who won the TV.

f) We sometimes go shopping not to buy anything, but just to _____.

g) It's fun learning about _____ words such as friendship and cupcake.

h) My aunt's dog Charlie is a real _____ when her cat Max is nearby.

i) Our new vacuum cleaner is very _____ compared to the old one.

j) A marsupial is an animal that carries its growing baby in its _____.

Brain Stretch

How many spelling words can you fit into one sentence and still make sense? Give it a try!

1. The letters **ou** and **ow** can have an **ow** sound or an **o** sound. Say the word out loud. Underline the words that have an **ow** sound. Circle the words that have an **o** sound.

a) plough	crowd	although	allow	glow
b) sprout	pillow	aloud	narrow	borrow
c) grouch	sparrow	cowl	snowball	shadow
d) bounce	throw	proud	shout	swallow

2. **Homophones** are words that sound the same, but are spelled differently and have different meanings. Say the word out loud. Draw a line from the word to its meaning.

a) peak	sweet thick spread made from fruit and sugar
b) peek	solitary or single; the only one
c) loan	sneak a quick look
d) lone	cloud of tiny water droplets in the air
e) jam	failed to reach, hit, or come into contact with something aimed at
f) jamb	lend something such as money or property
g) missed	very top of a mountain
h) mist	side surface of a doorway or window

1. Use the word list below to look for the words in the puzzle.

   Circle the word in the word search puzzle. Then cross out the word in the list.

F	O	U	N	T	A	I	N	S
A	B	I	G	R	O	U	C	H
L	O	H	O	U	R	O	Z	A
L	R	J	S	F	I	I	Y	L
O	R	C	N	Q	A	T	T	L
W	O	S	O	U	T	H	O	O
V	W	Y	W	F	G	F	W	W
O	Y	A	C	O	L	L	E	H
P	O	U	C	H	O	M	R	J
M	A	R	R	O	W	U	G	Z

allow	borrow	fountain	glow	grouch	hour
marrow	pouch	shallow	snow	south	tower

2. Write a word that ends in the same letters that are underlined below.

   Examples: **p<u>out</u>** **sc<u>out</u>** **g<u>own</u>** **t<u>own</u>** **c<u>ount</u>** **mo<u>unt</u>**

a) p<u>illow</u> _____

b) fr<u>own</u> _____

c) sc<u>our</u> _____

d) sc<u>owl</u> _____

e) h<u>ound</u> _____

f) fl<u>ower</u> _____

g) m<u>outh</u> _____

h) l<u>oud</u> _____

i) h<u>ouse</u> _____

Say each word out loud. Look at the different letters that make an **s** sound.

Copy and spell each word three times using colours of your choice.

1. brace   _____   _____   _____

2. saucer   _____   _____   _____

3. exciting   _____   _____   _____

4. collapse   _____   _____   _____

5. practice   _____   _____   _____

6. delicious   _____   _____   _____

7. absent   _____   _____   _____

8. disaster   _____   _____   _____

9. pharmacy _____   _____   _____

10. process   _____   _____   _____

Spelling Tip

The **s** sound can be spelled with the letters **s**, **ce**, **ci**, and **cy**.

absent	collapse	delicious	disaster	exciting
pharmacy	practice	process	saucer	unicycle

1. Fill in the blank using the best spelling word from the list.

a) My first attempt at making a cake was a complete _____.

b) Tom has hockey _____ every Monday and Thursday night.

c) Grandad made the most _____ homemade cinnamon bread today.

d) I found the teacup I wanted, but I can't find the matching _____.

e) Making homemade bread is a long, slow _____, but totally worth it.

f) Nanna has to pick up her medication at the _____ today.

g) If you build a tower of cards, it will eventually _____.

h) Dad said there will be an _____ surprise for us when we get home.

i) Kim was _____ from school today because she is sick.

j) Mack is learning to ride a _____. It's hard to balance!

Brain Stretch

How many spelling words can you fit into one sentence and still make sense? Give it a try!

1. Say the word out loud. Circle the words that do **not** have an *s* sound.

a) glance   organism   pastel   piece   reason

b) pose   fleece   wisdom   receive   pause

c) business   clothes   mercy   cookies   canvas

d) prism   claws   recite   present   since

2. **Homographs** are words that are spelled the same, but have different meanings and can sometimes sound different. Read the pronunciation key if there is one. Draw a line from the word to its meaning. You can use a dictionary, if needed.

a) close [clohss]   what is in something

b) close [clohz]   poor reason for having done something

c) patient   to lessen the blame for something

d) patient   shut something

e) excuse [ex-KYOOS]   someone being treated by a doctor

f) excuse [ex-KYOOZ]   happy

g) content [kuhn-TENT]   nearby

h) content [KON-tent]   able to tolerate or accept delays, problems, or suffering without becoming annoyed or anxious

1. Use the word list below to look for the words in the puzzle.

   Circle the word in the word search puzzle. Then cross out the word in the list.

T	S	T	E	N	C	I	L	P
H	P	R	E	C	I	P	E	R
I	E	G	L	A	N	C	E	I
S	A	H	C	P	I	I	P	V
T	C	R	I	G	S	B	R	A
L	E	O	T	F	T	R	E	C
E	Q	P	Y	A	G	A	S	Y
O	Y	X	P	N	H	S	S	H
T	C	I	R	C	U	S	B	J
S	P	I	C	Y	H	Q	G	Z

brass	circus	city	fancy	glance	peace
press	privacy	recipe	spicy	stencil	thistle

2. Write a word that rhymes with the word below. The word can be spelled differently.

a) rift _____

b) slice _____

c) dance _____

d) wrist _____

e) chase _____

f) dress _____

g) vest _____

h) juice _____

i) spider _____

Say each word out loud. Look at the different letters that make a *j* sound.

Copy and spell each word three times using colours of your choice.

1. January _____ _____ _____

2. adjust _____ _____ _____

3. reject _____ _____ _____

4. changing _____ _____ _____

5. general _____ _____ _____

6. biology _____ _____ _____

7. journey _____ _____ _____

8. mythology _____ _____ _____

9. magenta _____ _____ _____

10. giant _____ _____ _____

Spelling Tip

The *j* sound can be spelled with the letters *j*, *ge*, *gy*, and *gi*.

adjust	biology	changing	general	giant
January	journey	magenta	mythology	reject

1. Fill in the blank using the best spelling word from the list.

a) Our cat is fussy. She will often _____ a new type of food.

b) Greek and Roman _____ have very similar gods and goddesses.

c) My family loves to see the leaves _____ colour in the fall.

d) My great-grandfather was a _____ in World War II.

e) Kathy's new hamster went on a _____ into her dresser drawer.

f) Ravi's favourite colour is _____.

g) There is usually a lot of snow on the ground in _____ every winter.

h) It is hard to _____ to getting up early after summer vacation.

i) The _____ had a goose that laid golden eggs and Jack stole it.

j) _____ is the study of living things and their characteristics.

Brain Stretch

How many spelling words can you fit into one sentence and still make sense? Give it a try!

1. Say the word out loud. Circle the words that do **not** have a **j** sound.

a)	angle	angel	gift	jewellery	giant
b)	injured	gymnastics	organize	pigeon	finger
c)	gentle	janitor	garden	fridge	guard
d)	magic	geese	wiggle	range	ginger

2. The letters "ology" mean "the study of." When these letters are added to the end of a word, the beginning of the word tells what is being studied. Use a dictionary or the Internet to find the word meaning. Write a brief definition beside the word.

   Example: zoology   the study of animals, their bodies, and their behaviour

   a) criminology _____

   b) geology _____

   c) paleontology _____

   d) meteorology _____

   e) volcanology _____

   f) ornithology _____

   g) herpetology _____

   h) dermatology _____

adjust	biology	changing	general	giant
January	journey	magenta	mythology	reject

1. Write the correct spelling word from the list to match the clue.

a) A trip from one place to another; to travel somewhere _____

b) Dismiss as not good enough or not to one's taste _____

c) Affecting or concerning most people, places, or things; the commander of an army or a high ranking officer _____

d) Making or becoming different _____

e) A collection of myths, especially one belonging to a particular religious or cultural tradition _____

f) Light purplish-red colour _____

g) To adapt or become used to a new situation; to move something slightly to get the desired fit or appearance _____

h) The study of plants and animals, and their environments _____

i) The first month of the calendar year _____

j) An imaginary or mythical being of human form but superhuman size; of very great size or force _____

2. Do **not** use the spelling word list for this activity. Write a word that has the *j* sound made by the following letters. These letters can be anywhere in the word.

a) j _____   b) ge _____

c) gi _____   d) gy _____

Say each word out loud. Listen to the *f* sound the different letters make.

Copy and spell each word three times using colours of your choice.

1. drift _____ _____ _____

2. breakfast _____ _____ _____

3. enough _____ _____ _____

4. autograph _____ _____ _____

5. spherical _____ _____ _____

6. cliff _____ _____ _____

7. laughter _____ _____ _____

8. difficult _____ _____ _____

9. rough _____ _____ _____

10. cough _____ _____ _____

Brain Stretch

- Create a word search puzzle based on the spelling words.
- On a piece of paper, write a sentence using each spelling word.

autograph	**breakfast**	**cliffs**	**cough**	**difficult**
drift	**enough**	**laughter**	**rough**	**spherical**

1. Fill in the blank using the best spelling word from the list.

a) Two pieces of pepperoni pizza is _____ food for me.

b) We are having blueberry pancakes for _____ this morning.

c) The big hill in the forest is very _____ to climb on foot.

d) The toy boat my cousin was playing with began to _____ away.

e) My dad got the _____ of his favourite baseball player.

f) In England, there are huge white _____ made of chalk.

g) The green parrot erupts in loud _____ whenever it's very happy.

h) Sandpaper's _____ surface is used to make wood smooth.

i) I always have a _____ when I catch a cold.

j) A globe is a _____ object and so is an orange.

Brain Stretch

How many spelling words can you fit into one sentence and still make sense? Give it a try!

A **metaphor** is a figure of speech that compares two things that are not alike but have something in common. Metaphors compare by saying something **is** something else. Metaphors do **not** use the words **like** or **as** to compare.

*Example: The stars **are** sparkling diamonds in the night sky.*

1. Write a metaphor to complete the sentence. Remember not to use **like** or **as**.

   a) My toes are _____ when I play in the snow.

   b) The sun is a _____ in the evening sky.

   c) Freshy baked bread is _____ to my nose.

   d) My bedroom is a _____ when I'm feeling sad.

   e) Gently falling snowflakes are _____.

   f) The stormy sea is _____.

   g) Thunder is _____.

2. A **synonym** is a word that means the same as another word. Circle the synonym for the bolded word.

   a) **rough**   dirty   scratchy   b) **tough**   slippery   strong

3. An **antonym** is a word that has the opposite meaning of another word. Circle the antonym for the bolded word.

   a) **laugh**   cry   angry   b) **phony**   fake   real

1. Use the word list below to look for the words in the puzzle.

   Circle the word in the word search puzzle. Then cross out the word in the list.

S	T	U	F	F	I	N	G	F
A	P	H	I	D	M	N	O	A
K	H	Y	P	H	E	N	P	B
M	O	F	M	D	T	S	H	U
U	N	L	A	U	G	H	E	L
F	E	O	M	W	T	X	R	O
F	L	U	F	F	Y	D	F	U
L	Y	P	H	O	T	O	I	S
E	N	Y	M	P	H	M	S	J
R	T	R	O	U	G	H	G	Z

aphid	fabulous	fluffy	gopher	hyphen	laugh
muffler	nymph	phone	photo	trough	stuffing

2. Write a word that rhymes with the word below. The word does not have to be spelled the same.

   a) laugh _____   b) rough _____   c) fake _____

   d) feel _____   e) fudge _____   f) phone _____

   g) sphinx _____   h) finch _____   i) file _____

Say each word out loud. Listen for the different sounds the digraphs make.

Copy and spell each word three times using colours of your choice.

1. theatre _____ _____ _____

2. whisper _____ _____ _____

3. exchange _____ _____ _____

4. channel _____ _____ _____

5. fashion _____ _____ _____

6. whirl _____ _____ _____

7. approach _____ _____ _____

8. shadow _____ _____ _____

9. chimney _____ _____ _____

10. thunder _____ _____ _____

Brain Stretch

- Create a word search puzzle based on the spelling words.
- On a piece of paper, write a sentence using each spelling word.

| approach | chimney | establish | exchange | fashion |
| shadow | theatre | thunder | whirls | whisper |

1. Fill in the blank using the best spelling word from the list.

a) When the wind blows, it _____ the leaves in the corner of the house.

b) My sister is very interested in the latest trends for _____.

c) Our dog hides under the bed whenever he hears _____.

d) Ants work hard to _____ a large working colony underground.

e) A cloud can make a _____ down on the ground on a sunny day.

f) I have to _____ the pants my aunt bought me. They're too small.

g) We can see the big sign for the fun fair as we _____ the school.

h) A raccoon had babies inside our _____ last spring.

i) My friend Carrie and I are going to see a movie at the _____.

j) We have to _____ so we don't wake my baby brother up.

Brain Stretch

How many spelling words can you fit into one sentence and still make sense? Give it a try!

Spelling Week 21 – Word Study

1. Write the correct digraph letters in the word. Use **ch**, **sh**, **th**, or **wh**. Say the word out loud to check it.

a) lun_____

b) _____ought

c) _____ingles

d) four_____

e) fi_____

f) _____ange

g) _____roat

h) _____ether

i) _____ing

j) _____isper

k) spla_____

l) _____imp

2. How many words can you make? Use only **ch, sh, th,** and **wh** and the letters given to make the words. Say the word out loud to make sure it's a real word. Write your words on the line.

Examples: am   wham   sham

a) ip _____

b) ick _____

c) wi _____

d) at _____

e) en _____

f) in _____

g) eat _____

h) ose _____

| approach | chimney | establish | exchange | fashion |
| shadow | theatre | thunder | whirls | whisper |

1. Write the correct spelling word from the list to match the clue.

a) To move or cause to move rapidly round and round _____

b) Give something and receive something of the same kind or value in return _____

c) Loud rumbling or crashing sound heard after a lightning flash _____

d) Come near or nearer to someone or something in distance or time _____

e) Set up a business or organization on a firm or permanent foundation; give something a good start _____

f) A popular trend, especially in styles of clothing and accessories _____

g) A vertical pipe or channel that conducts smoke and gas from a fire up through the roof and into the air outside _____

h) Dark shape or area produced by something coming between light and a surface _____

i) Building or outdoor area in which plays are performed or movies are shown _____

j) To talk very quietly using the breath but not using the vocal cords _____

Say each word out loud. Listen to the sounds each consonant blend makes.

Copy and spell each word three times using colours of your choice.

1. instruction _____ _____ _____

2. sprint _____ _____ _____

3. instrument _____ _____ _____

4. subscribe _____ _____ _____

5. sprig _____ _____ _____

6. astronaut _____ _____ _____

7. describe _____ _____ _____

8. splatter _____ _____ _____

9. splinter _____ _____ _____

10. straight _____ _____ _____

Brain Stretch

- Create a word search puzzle based on the spelling words.
- On a piece of paper, write a sentence using each spelling word.

astronaut	**describe**	**distrust**	**instruction**	**splatter**
splinter	**sprig**	**sprint**	**straight**	**subscribe**

1. Fill in the blank using the best spelling word from the list.

a) Every day, my brother and I _____ to the mailbox to get the mail.

b) Rani wants to be an _____ when she grows up.

c) My little sister brought in a _____ of cedar leaves for my mom.

d) I want to _____ to LEGO Magazine so I can see all the new sets.

e) Leon got a big _____ from his neighbour's wooden fence.

f) Our homework is to _____ the greatest adventure we've ever had.

g) We need to read the _____ sheet to put together the bookcase.

h) I need to find my ruler so I can draw a nice _____ line.

i) Lane wanted to play an _____, so she chose the drums.

j) Stand back when cooking bacon so grease doesn't _____ on you.

Brain Stretch

How many spelling words can you fit into one sentence and still make sense?
Give it a try!

Write a short story using as many of these new words as you can.

scrape	**scratch**	**scream**	**splinter**	**split**
sprig	**sprinkle**	**stranger**	**stroller**	**structure**

_____

_____

_____

_____

_____

_____

_____

_____

_____

_____

1. Use the word list below to look for the words in the puzzle.

   Circle the word in the puzzle. Then cross out the word in the list.

S	P	R	I	N	T	P	R	S
C	D	E	S	T	R	O	Y	P
R	S	S	T	S	S	V	Q	R
A	P	P	R	C	P	U	T	A
P	R	L	A	R	L	S	O	I
B	U	A	Y	U	I	K	E	N
P	C	S	T	B	T	D	K	I
W	E	H	S	C	R	U	F	F
K	D	I	S	P	L	A	Y	J
D	I	S	T	R	I	C	T	Z

display   **destroy**   **district**   **scrap**   **scrub**   **scruff**

splash   **split**   **sprain**   **sprint**   **spruce**   **stray**

2. Write **scr, spl, spr,** or **str** to make a word. Make sure to say the word out loud to check it.

a) _____unch   b) _____eet   c) _____itz

d) _____eam   e) _____ub   f) _____at

g) _____ipt   h) _____ayer   i) _____ength

j) _____out   k) _____ipes   l) _____ead

When the letter *r* follows a vowel, it changes the sound of the vowel.

Examples: cat car   box born   gift girl   vet verb   cut curl

Say each word out loud. Listen to how the vowels are pronounced. Copy and spell each word three times using colours of your choice.

1. sailor   _____   _____   _____

2. thirsty   _____   _____   _____

3. chapter   _____   _____   _____

4. urban   _____   _____   _____

5. adverb   _____   _____   _____

6. squirm   _____   _____   _____

7. doctor   _____   _____   _____

8. appear   _____   _____   _____

9. pearl   _____   _____   _____

10. urgent   _____   _____   _____

adverb	appear	chapter	doctor	pearl
sailor	squirm	thirsty	urban	urgent

1. Fill in the blank using the best spelling word from the list.

a) My Uncle Nick was a _____ during World War II.

b) We live in an _____ area, which means we live in a city.

c) Hold the paper close to a light bulb to make the secret message _____.

d) I'm reading a very exciting _____ in my book!

e) Cathy's mother had an oyster and there was a small _____ in it.

f) Tim's _____ said he was too sick to go to school this week.

g) An _____ is a word that describes a verb, such as "gently patted."

h) When a tense part comes in a movie, it makes me _____.

i) It's hot outside, so we are all very _____ and need water.

j) The caller said it was _____ but they weren't telling the truth.

Brain Stretch

How many spelling words can you fit into one sentence and still make sense? Give it a try!

The letter combinations listed below all make an *er* sound, however, that's not always true. The same letter combination can make different sounds. For example, in the word *work*, the *or* as an *er* sound, but in the word *pork* it does not. Also, when a vowel is followed by a **consonant + e, i,** or **y**, the vowel usually says its name (*a, e, i, o,* or *u*). When that happens, the same combination of letters don't have an *er* sound, such as in the words *her* and *here*.

1. Write a word with an *er* sound made by the given letters. Then write a word with the same letter combination that does not make an *er* sound.

   Examples: first hire   pearl gear   fur pour   were here   tern steer   work pork

   a) ir _____

   b) er _____

   c) ur _____

   d) or _____

   e) ear _____

2. **Homophones** are words that sound the same, but are spelled differently. Read the word. Write its homophone on the line.

   Examples: reed   read   red   read   blew   blue

   a) allowed _____   b) berry _____   c) scent _____

   d) foul _____   e) grown _____   f) need _____

   g) links _____   h) main _____   i) mussel _____

   j) padded _____   k) pause _____   l) plain _____

| adverb | appear | chapter | doctor | pearl |
| sailor | squirm | thirsty | urban | urgent |

1. Write the correct spelling word from the list to match the clue.

a) Describing a state or situation requiring immediate
action or attention _____

b) In need of a drink of water or other liquid _____

c) Hard shiny mass formed in the shell of an oyster
and highly prized as a gem _____

d) Come into sight; become visible; be made clear _____

e) To wriggle or twist the body from side to side from
nervousness or discomfort _____

f) Word or phrase that tells how an action was done _____

g) Of or relating to the city _____

h) A main division of a book, usually with number and title _____

i) Health professional who takes care of sick people and
prescribes treatment and medication _____

j) A person whose job it is to work on a fishing boat or
a navy ship _____

The letter *r* changes the way vowels sound, such as in the words **fog** and **fort**.

The letters **or** and **ore** usually make the same sound.

Examples: torn   tore   fork   forest

The letters **ar** and **are** usually sound different.

Examples: car   care   star   stare

Say each word out loud. Listen to the sound of the vowels before the *r*.

Copy and spell each word three times using colours of your choice.

1. scared   _____ _____ _____

2. ignore   _____ _____ _____

3. apartment _____ _____ _____

4. flare   _____ _____ _____

5. artist   _____ _____ _____

6. factor   _____ _____ _____

7. store   _____ _____ _____

8. snore   _____ _____ _____

9. monitor   _____ _____ _____

10. editor   _____ _____ _____

| apartment | artist | aware | editor | factor |
| flare | ignore | scared | snore | store |

1. Fill in the blank using the best spelling word from the list.

a) Our dog Blue tends to _____ loudly when he's sleeping.

b) Cats usually _____ people unless they want something from them.

c) The boat's engine stalled. The captain sent up a _____ to get help.

d) My grandparents sold their house and moved into a nice _____.

e) The weather will be a _____ in deciding where we have our party.

f) Our three dogs are all _____ of kids in Halloween costumes.

g) Phil can draw things that look real. He's a very good _____.

h) We are going to the hardware _____ to buy a new hammer for me!

i) That cat is very _____ of the tiny mouse hiding in the grass nearby.

j) Aunt Becky is an _____ who works for the local newspaper.

Brain Stretch

How many spelling words can you fit into one sentence and still make sense? Give it a try!

Spelling Week 24 – Word Study

1. On the lines below, write these words in alphabetical order.

| shark | park | ignore | torn | chore | rare |

a) _____   b) _____   c) _____

d) _____   e) _____   f) _____

2. Write a short sentence using the word below. Check your punctation.

a) spark _____

b) core _____

c) mark _____

d) fork _____

e) scare _____

f) storm _____

g) bark _____

h) tore _____

i) dare _____

1. Use the word list below to look for the words in the puzzle.

   Circle the word in the word search puzzle. Then cross out the word in the list.

F	A	R	M	E	R	A	S	B
L	S	O	R	T	E	D	M	O
A	R	P	E	C	O	O	A	R
R	I	S	N	O	R	E	R	D
E	G	C	E	U	S	S	T	E
A	N	A	R	S	E	E	R	R
H	O	R	S	E	P	D	W	E
W	R	Y	P	Y	I	A	O	H
I	E	U	A	I	K	M	R	J
B	A	R	K	I	N	G	E	K

barking	**border**	**farmer**	**flare**	**horse**	**ignore**
park	**scary**	**smart**	**snore**	**sorted**	**wore**

2. Write a word that rhymes with the word below. The word does not have to be spelled the same.

   a) bore _____   b) spark _____   c) corn_____

   d) stare _____   e) short _____   f) tarp _____

   g) cord _____   h) caret _____   i) spork _____

Say each word out loud. Listen for the words that sound the same.

Copy and spell each word three times using colours of your choice.

1. wood   _____   _____   _____

2. their   _____   _____   _____

3. cent   _____   _____   _____

4. higher   _____   _____   _____

5. pause   _____   _____   _____

6. would   _____   _____   _____

7. scent   _____   _____   _____

8. there   _____   _____   _____

9. hire   _____   _____   _____

10. paws   _____   _____   _____

Brain Stretch

- Create a word search puzzle based on the spelling words.
- On a piece of paper, write a sentence using each spelling word.

cent	higher	hire	pause	paws
scent	their	there	wood	would

1. Fill in the blank using the best spelling word from the list.

a) Hansel and Gretel's father cut _____ for a living.

b) The coach told us to stand over _____ while he chooses teams.

c) My brother's cat is black with white _____ and her name is Socks.

d) Grandma says when she was a girl candy cost only one _____.

e) I _____ love to see the fireworks at the park this weekend.

f) Our neighbours have _____ Christmas decorations up already!

g) Sharon is hoping the music store will _____ her after her interview.

h) The _____ of lilacs is one of my favourite childhood memories.

i) Mom keeps telling Dad to raise the painting just a little bit _____.

j) There's a four-beat _____ in the song I'm learning on the piano.

Brain Stretch

How many spelling words can you fit into one sentence and still make sense? Give it a try!

1. **Homophones** are words that sound the same, but are spelled differently and have different meanings. Read the word. Write its homophone on the line.

a) reign _____

b) choose _____

c) scene _____

d) side _____

e) steel _____

f) piece _____

g) heard _____

h) stair _____

i) yoke _____

j) we've _____

k) vary _____

l) throne _____

2. **Homographs** are words that are spelled the same, but have different meanings and can sometimes sound different. Read the pronunciation key if there is one. Draw a line from the word to its meaning. You can use a dictionary, if needed.

a) dove [duhv]   turn a key to operate a clockwork object

b) dove [dohv]   let go from a job

c) fire   to make something perfect

d) fire   air current blowing from a specific direction

e) perfect [purFIKT]   plump cooing bird with a small head, short legs

f) perfect [purFEKT]   as good as possible

g) wind [whind]   plunged head first into water

h) wind [whynd]   burning that gives off light, heat, and smoke

1. Use the word list below to look for the words in the puzzle.

   Circle the word in the word search puzzle. Then cross out the word in the list.

P	A	D	D	E	D	A	X	M
A	K	I	D	L	M	N	R	I
T	N	M	I	S	T	O	A	S
T	O	J	C	F	I	I	Y	S
E	W	R	O	U	T	E	S	E
D	S	O	W	P	H	Q	R	D
V	H	E	R	D	G	D	O	E
R	A	I	S	E	I	L	O	H
I	S	L	N	O	S	E	T	J
H	E	A	R	D	Y	U	W	Z

heard	herd	knows	missed	mist	nose
padded	patted	raise	rays	root	route

2. Draw a line to the meaning of the homophone below.

   a) steal   attached or fastened with string or cord

   b) steel   take something without paying for it

   c) tied   rising and falling of the sea with the moon and sun

   d) tide   hard, strong grey or bluish metal

Spelling Week 1 – Test

Name: _____

Listen to the spelling words. Print each spelling word.

1. _____   6. _____

2. _____   7. _____

3. _____   8. _____

4. _____   9. _____

5. _____   10. _____

Bonus

1. _____   2. _____

Spelling Week 2 – Test

Name: _____

Listen to the spelling words. Print each spelling word.

1. _____   6. _____

2. _____   7. _____

3. _____   8. _____

4. _____   9. _____

5. _____   10. _____

Bonus

1. _____   2. _____

Spelling Week 3 – Test

Name: _____

Listen to the spelling words. Print each spelling word.

1. _____   6. _____

2. _____   7. _____

3. _____   8. _____

4. _____   9. _____

5. _____   10. _____

Bonus

1. _____   2. _____

Spelling Week 4 – Test

Name: _____

Listen to the spelling words. Print each spelling word.

1. _____   6. _____

2. _____   7. _____

3. _____   8. _____

4. _____   9. _____

5. _____   10. _____

Bonus

1. _____   2. _____

Spelling Week 5 – Test

Name: _____

Listen to the spelling words. Print each spelling word.

1. _____   6. _____

2. _____   7. _____

3. _____   8. _____

4. _____   9. _____

5. _____   10. _____

Bonus

1. _____   2. _____

Spelling Week 6 – Test

Name: _____

Listen to the spelling words. Print each spelling word.

1. _____   6. _____

2. _____   7. _____

3. _____   8. _____

4. _____   9. _____

5. _____   10. _____

Bonus

1. _____   2. _____

Spelling Week 7 – Test

Name: _____

Listen to the spelling words. Print each spelling word.

1. _____   6. _____

2. _____   7. _____

3. _____   8. _____

4. _____   9. _____

5. _____   10. _____

Bonus

1. _____   2. _____

Spelling Week 8 – Test

Name: _____

Listen to the spelling words. Print each spelling word.

1. _____   6. _____

2. _____   7. _____

3. _____   8. _____

4. _____   9. _____

5. _____   10. _____

Bonus

1. _____   2. _____

Spelling Week 9 – Test

Name: _____

Listen to the spelling words. Print each spelling word.

1. _____   6. _____

2. _____   7. _____

3. _____   8. _____

4. _____   9. _____

5. _____   10. _____

Bonus

1. _____   2. _____

Spelling Week 10 – Test

Name: _____

Listen to the spelling words. Print each spelling word.

1. _____   6. _____

2. _____   7. _____

3. _____   8. _____

4. _____   9. _____

5. _____   10. _____

Bonus

1. _____   2. _____

Spelling Week 11 – Test

Name: _____

Listen to the spelling words. Print each spelling word.

1. _____   6. _____

2. _____   7. _____

3. _____   8. _____

4. _____   9. _____

5. _____   10. _____

Bonus

1. _____   2. _____

- -

Spelling Week 12 – Test

Name: _____

Listen to the spelling words. Print each spelling word.

1. _____   6. _____

2. _____   7. _____

3. _____   8. _____

4. _____   9. _____

5. _____   10. _____

Bonus

1. _____   2. _____

Spelling Week 13 – Test

Name: _____

Listen to the spelling words. Print each spelling word.

1. _____   6. _____

2. _____   7. _____

3. _____   8. _____

4. _____   9. _____

5. _____   10. _____

Bonus

1. _____   2. _____

- -

Spelling Week 14 – Test

Name: _____

Listen to the spelling words. Print each spelling word.

1. _____   6. _____

2. _____   7. _____

3. _____   8. _____

4. _____   9. _____

5. _____   10. _____

Bonus

1. _____   2. _____

Spelling Week 15 – Test

Name: _____

Listen to the spelling words. Print each spelling word.

1. _____   6. _____

2. _____   7. _____

3. _____   8. _____

4. _____   9. _____

5. _____   10. _____

Bonus

1. _____   2. _____

Spelling Week 16 – Test

Name: _____

Listen to the spelling words. Print each spelling word.

1. _____   6. _____

2. _____   7. _____

3. _____   8. _____

4. _____   9. _____

5. _____   10. _____

Bonus

1. _____   2. _____

Spelling Week 17 – Test

Name: _____

Listen to the spelling words. Print each spelling word.

1. _____   6. _____

2. _____   7. _____

3. _____   8. _____

4. _____   9. _____

5. _____   10. _____

Bonus

1. _____   2. _____

Spelling Week 18 – Test

Name: _____

Listen to the spelling words. Print each spelling word.

1. _____   6. _____

2. _____   7. _____

3. _____   8. _____

4. _____   9. _____

5. _____   10. _____

Bonus

1. _____   2. _____

Spelling Week 19 – Test   Name: _____

Listen to the spelling words. Print each spelling word.

1. _____   6. _____

2. _____   7. _____

3. _____   8. _____

4. _____   9. _____

5. _____   10. _____

Bonus

1. _____   2. _____

Spelling Week 20 – Test   Name: _____

Listen to the spelling words. Print each spelling word.

1. _____   6. _____

2. _____   7. _____

3. _____   8. _____

4. _____   9. _____

5. _____   10. _____

Bonus

1. _____   2. _____

Spelling Week 21 – Test

Name: _____

Listen to the spelling words. Print each spelling word.

1. _____   6. _____

2. _____   7. _____

3. _____   8. _____

4. _____   9. _____

5. _____   10. _____

Bonus

1. _____   2. _____

Spelling Week 22 – Test

Name: _____

Listen to the spelling words. Print each spelling word.

1. _____   7. _____

2. _____   8. _____

3. _____   9. _____

4. _____   10. _____

5. _____   11. _____

6. _____   12. _____

Spelling Week 23 – Test

Name: _____

Listen to the spelling words. Print each spelling word.

1. _____   6. _____

2. _____   7. _____

3. _____   8. _____

4. _____   9. _____

5. _____   10. _____

Bonus

1. _____   2. _____

Spelling Week 24 – Test

Name: _____

Listen to the spelling words. Print each spelling word.

1. _____   6. _____

2. _____   7. _____

3. _____   8. _____

4. _____   9. _____

5. _____   10. _____

Bonus

1. _____   2. _____

Spelling Week 25 – Test

Name: _____

Listen to the spelling words. Print each spelling word.

1. _____

2. _____

3. _____

4. _____

5. _____

6. _____

7. _____

8. _____

9. _____

10. _____

Bonus

1. _____

2. _____

Answers

Spelling Week 1 – Words with a Short *a* Sound, pp. 2–3
1. a) lavender b) graphic c) cactus d) forecast e) elasticity f)
abacus g) hyena h) discard i) Italy
j) bamboo

Spelling Week 1 – Word Study, p. 4
1. a) graphic b) hyena c) abacus d) Italy e) forecast f) cactus
g) bamboo h) lavender
2. a) Italy b) abacus c) hyena d) bamboo e) forecast f)
cactus g) graphic h) lavender
3. a) apple b) pants c) smacked d) after

Spelling Week 1 – Word Study, p. 5
1. a) cactus b) Italy c) lavender d) elasticity e) graphic f)
bamboo g) forecast h) hyena i) abacus
j) discard
2. a) slack, fast, calf b) tackle, blanket, habitat c) laugh,
splash, crab

Spelling Week 2 – Words with a Short *e* Sound, pp. 6–7
1. a) pelican b) Neptune c) kennel d) melody e) insect f)
active g) ointment h) oxygen i) level
j) pretzel

Spelling Week 2 – Word Study, p. 8
1. a) special, propel, better, felt b) lending, fresh, weather,
spelll c) fender, lemming, wealth
d) barrette, spread, elephant e) friend, kept, crest
2. a) pelican b) kennel c) melody d) ointment
3. Sample answers: A table should be level or things will roll
off. My hamster's cage has a level where he sleeps, a level
where he eats, and a level where he can run on his exercise
wheel.

Spelling Week 2 – Word Study, p. 9
1. a) active b) kennel c) pretzel d) melody e) Neptune f) level
g) insect h) ointment i) oxygen
j) pelican
2. Sample answers: a) fell, smell, spell, swell, tell b) health
c) kept

Spelling Week 3 – Words with a Short *i* Sound, pp. 10–11
1. a) asterisk b) hesitant c) knitting d) jingle e) comic f)
millionth g) impossible h) picnic i) distract j) fantastic

Spelling Week 3 – Word Study, p. 12
1. a) impossible b) picnic c) fitness
2. a) build b) mist c) which d) guilt e) lynx
3. a) 2 syllables b) 5 syllables c) 2 syllables
4. Sample answers: a) willed, filled, billed, gild, guild, build,
killed, grilled, spilled b) bit, mitt, kit, knit, nit, fit, sit c) sift, lift,
rift, miffed d) kitten, bitten e) glitter, bitter, sitter, fitter f) flip,
lip, clip, drip, ship, hip, nip, rip, whip, trip

Spelling Week 3 – Word Study, p. 13
1.

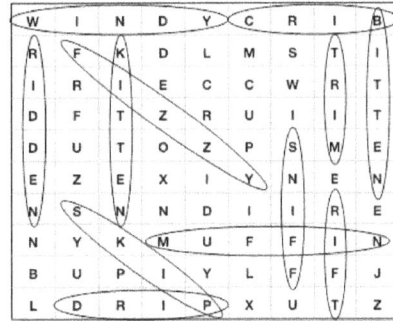

2. a) knitting b) picnic c) distract d) jingle e) millionth f)
asterisk

**Spelling Week 4 – Words with a Short *o* Sound, pp.
14–15**
1. a) novel b) fond c) flock d) biology e) cousin f) doctor g)
dropped h) fashion i) hospital j) model

Spelling Week 4 – Word Study, p. 16
1. a) doctor b) flock c) model d) fond
2. Sample answers: a) stopped, popped, flopped, cropped
b) sock, clock, knock, shock, crock, talk, walk c) pond,
bond, frond, wand d) lot, hot, got, rot, shot, trot, fought,
ought, caught
e) loss, moss, sauce, floss, gloss, cross f) love, above,
shove g) sport, court, fort, torte h) lop, hop, top, stop, shop,
crop, flop i) song, wrong
3. a) glossy, tonic, softly b) tropical, cross, blond c) pocket,
strong, fossil

Spelling Week 4 – Word Study, p. 17
1. a) novel b) biology c_ model d) hospital e) doctor f)
dropped g) fond h) flock i) cousin j) fashion
2. a) fashion d) model c) cousin d) biology e) doctor f)
hospital

**Spelling Week 5 – Words with a Short *u* Sound, pp.
18–19**
1. a) crumb b) submarine c) tumble d) dull e) bundle f)
mustard g) volunteer h) fungus i) cluster
j) August

Spelling Week 5 – Word Study, p. 20
1. a) cloud, through b) bounce, cough c) shout, flute d)
though, guest
2. Sample answers: a) fully, bully, gully b) glove, shove, love
d) puff, fluff, muff, cuff, scuff
d) puddle, muddle e) stumble, tumble, crumble, bumble,
rumble f) rough, tough, enough
3. a) mustard b) volunteer c) tumble d) fungus e) crumb f)
august g) cluster h) submarine i) dull

Spelling Week 5 – Word Study, p. 21

1.

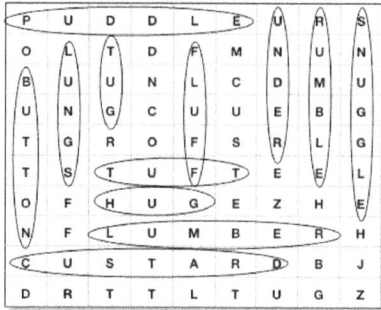

2. Sample answers: a) ton, shun, fun, one, done, won, run
b) tough, cuff, scuff, muff, fluff
c) yummy, mummy, dummy d) humble, bumble, tumble, stumble, rumble e) thunder, wonder, under, plunder f) lumpy, stumpy, dumpy, bumpy

Spelling Week 6 – Words with a Long *a* Sound, pp. 22–23

1. a) container b) daisy c) hurricane d) greatest e) indicate f) afraid g) arrange h) canine
i) complain j) Ancient (it's okay if they don't use a capital)

Spelling Week 6 – Word Study, p. 24

1. a) state, rake, scale b) shake, crazy, grate c) paste, train, clay d) parade, quake, sway e) pace, fair, aim
2. Sample answers: table, chair, slate, bookcase, crayons, paper, crate, paints, paintbrushes, trays, plates, laces, cables, faces, cases, pencil cases
3. Stories will vary. You may wish to ask some children to share with the class or with a partner.

Spelling Week 6 – Word Study, p. 25

1.

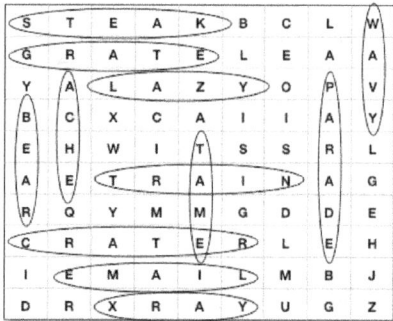

2. Sample answers: a) care, bear, rare, air, stare, stair, share, dare, pear, pare, fair b) take, sake, fake, make, ache, lake, rake c) came, tame, lame, fame, shame, frame, blame, game d) taste, waist, paste, paced, raced, aced, erased e) day, say, ray, lay, way, hay, stay, pay, delay, fray, pray, prey f) gain, main, lane, rain, sane, cane, again, train, plane, plain, strain, crane, pain

Spelling Week 7 – Words with a Long *e* Sound, pp. 26–27

1. a) reason b) eager c) museum d) breathe e) increase f) beetle g) eagle h) chief i) appeal
j) adhere

Spelling Week 7 – Word Study, p. 28

1. a) museum b) eager c) adhere d) appeal e) increase f) chief g) reason h) breathe i) eagle
2. a) shield, mean, donkey b) belief, even, greet c) tweek, bunny, treat d) creek, valley e) speak, meek, fairy
3. a) cart/wheel, blue/berry, earth/quake b) sea/star, fire/works, head/band c) ear/lobe, finger/nail, sting/ray d) nose/bleed, eye/lash, pony/tail

Spelling Week 7 – Word Study, p. 29

1. a) chief b) eagle c) beetle d) increase e) reason f) eager g) breathe h) adhere i) appeal
j) museum
2. Sample answers: a) feed, speech, seek, leek, keen, seen, been, free, greet, greedy b) field, believe, belief, brief, chief, niece, priest, siege, achieve, piece c) funny, bunny, runny, sunny, monkey, donkey, galley, alley, valley d) weak, dear, fear, gear, leaf, steal, meal, real, deal, heal, seal, zeal, appeal, squeal, read

Spelling Week 8 – Words with a Long *i* Sound, pp. 30–31

1. a) feline b) cacti c) define d) entire e) graphite f) dried g) delight h) climb i) combine j) assign

Spelling Week 8 – Word Study, p. 32

1. a) twine, sigh, lightning b) flight, smile, cry c) sign, rhyme, write d) grime, cycle, white e) spice, dried, hire
2. a) backbone b) timid
3. a) cacti b) combined c) assigned d) climb e) wipe

Spelling Week 8 – Word Study, p. 33

1.

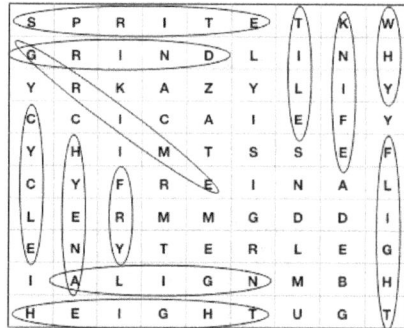

2. Sample answers: a) line, spine, mine, wine, whine, fine b) like, trike, bike, pike c) lie, die, cry, sigh, dry, fry, spy, shy, try d) while, file, mile, bile, smile, pile, trial e) flight, white, right, write, bright, might, sprite, fright, kite, bite, site, sight f) wide, glide, cried, fried, dried, pride

Spelling Week 9 – Words with a Long *o* Sound, pp. 34–35

1. a) motion b) ocean c) frozen d) calico e) golden f) Mexico g) radio h) gopher i) locate j) polar

Spelling Week 9 – Word Study, p. 36

1. A long time <u>ago</u>, there was a mean lion who was king of the jungle. One day, a little mouse ran across the lion's paw when he was sleeping and the lion <u>woke</u> up. He caught the mouse by the tail. "Please let me <u>go</u>!" cried the mouse. The lion said, "Why should I let you <u>go</u>?" The mouse said, "If you let me <u>go</u>,

one day I may be able to help you." The lion laughed. "How could a tiny mouse like you ever help a big lion like me?" he said. "<u>Although</u> I am small," said the mouse, "I just might surprise you." The lion thought it was <u>so</u> funny that he let the mouse <u>go</u> free. The mouse thanked him and ran off.

One day, some men came into the jungle and captured the lion in a big net. The lion roared in fear, but there was <u>no</u> way he could get out. The men left the lion tied to a tree while they hunted for more animals to capture. The little mouse heard the lion roaring and ran to him. The tiny mouse used his teeth to gnaw a <u>hole</u> in the net large enough for the lion to escape. The lion thanked the mouse and ran off. From that day forward, the lion <u>no</u> longer judged an animal <u>solely</u> by its size.
2. a) miss b) thawed
3. hung loosely and gracefully

Spelling Week 9 – Word Study, p. 37
1. a) gopher b) calico c) ocean d) motion e) golden f) polar g) Mexico h) locate i) frozen j) radio
2. Sample answers: a) toe, foe, hoe, doe, oboe b) float, boat, coat, goat, moat, stoat, oat, groan, toast, goal, loaf, load, road, roam c) grow, glow, flow, know, show, slow, snow, growth, narrow, sparrow, furrow, barrow, tomorrow d) go, no, so, banjo, bonus, focus, comb, total, piano, solo, trio (Note: Words with a consonant + e are also acceptable. Sample answers: bone, tone, phone, alone, stroke, stole, store, etc.

Spelling Week 10 – Words with a Long *u* Sound, pp. 38–39
1. a) Casual or casual b) annual c) cashew d) rescue e) jewel f) tissue g) graduate h) uniform
i) feud j) genuine

Spelling Week 10 – Word Study, p. 40
1. a) rescue, cue, unite b) university, menu, yule c) chew, music, argue d) rescue, view, unique
2. Sample answers: The human eye has a black pupil. My teacher says I am a very good pupil.
3. Sample answers: I try hard to communicate with my baby sister, but she doesn't talk yet. My best friend and I communicate very well in our secret language.

Spelling Week 10 – Word Study, p. 41
1.

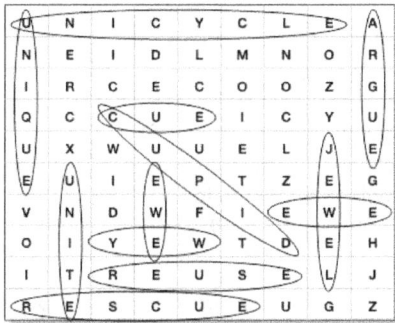

Spelling Week 11 – Words with *y* as Long *i* and Long *e* Sounds, pp. 42–43
1. a) balcony b) archery c) apology d) hydrogen e) identify f) kayak g) hydrate h) delivery i) colony j) cyclone

Spelling Week 11 – Word Study, p. 44
1. a) cyclone b) kayak c) archery d) identify e) delivery f) balcony
2. a) book + shelf, day + dream b) some + one, body + guard c) straw + berry, fire + fighter

Spelling Week 11 – Word Study, p. 45
1. a) colony b) hydrate c) archery d) cyclone e) apology f) delivery g) identify h) balcony
i) hydrogen j) kayak
2. Sample answers: I type my school work on my laptop. An oxeye daisy is a type of wildflower.

Spelling Week 12 – Contractions, pp. 46–47
1. a) you're b) couldn't c) I've d) it's e) won't f) He'll g) she'd h) haven't i) We've j) they'll

Spelling Week 12 – Word Study, p. 48
1. a) circle "willn't"; won't b) circle "cann't"; can't c) circle "willn't"; won't d) circle "cant"; can't
e) circle "Donot"; Don't f) circle "Hasnot"; Hasn't
2. a) could not b) has not c) we are d) she had or she would e) that is f) do not g) cannot h) will not
i) you will j) he is or he has

Spelling Week 12 – Word Study, p. 49
1. a) It's not what you look at that matters, but what you see. b) Isn't it amazing how a person who was once a stranger can suddenly become your best friend?

Spelling Week 13 – Double Consonants, pp. 50–51
1. a) carried b) arrange c) batter d) annoying e) collect f) babble g) fizz h) shell i) fluff j) grass

Spelling Week 13 – Word Study, p. 52
1. a) grabbed, grabbing b) knitted, knitting c) crossed, crossing d) planted, planting e) preferred, preferring
2. a) X; showing b) ✔ c) ✔ d) X; washing e) X; travelled f) X; melting g) ✔ h) X; walking

Spelling Week 13 – Word Study, p. 53
1.

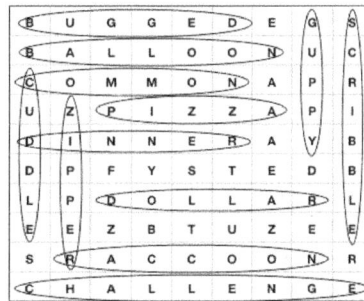

2. Sample answers: a) ball, wall, tall, crawl, mall, drawl, call, shawl b) bitter, sitter, critter, litter, twitter c) spill, fill, chill, grill, pill, sill, frill, bill, will d) fatter, patter, spatter, splatter, shatter, batter e) loss, boss, cross, floss f) any, many g) runny, funny, sunny, money, honey h) jell, spell, bell, fell, shell, well, smell i) fill, will, sill, mill, until, spill, shrill, thrill

Answers

Spelling Week 14 – Words with Silent Letters, pp. 54–55
1. a) drizzle b) escape c) bruise d) design e) caught f) crumb
g) glisten h) honest i) salmon
j) knead

Spelling Week 14 – Word Study, p. 56
1. a) through, tube, honest b) muscle, unique, fuse c)
school, argue, talk d) true, knight, listen
e) calf, thumb, gnome
2. a) fare b) twine c) shine d) cute e) stare f) scrape g) fade
h) dime
3. Sample answer: When I add an **e**, the vowel changes
from a short sound to a long sound.
4. a) L b) S c) L d) L e) S f) L g) S h) L

Spelling Week 14 – Word Study, p. 57
1. a) knead b) salmon c) design d) caught e) glisten f) bruise
g) drizzle h) crumb i) escape
j) honest
2. Sample answers: a) write, wrong, wriggle, wrap, wrist,
wrinkle, wreck, wreath, wren, wrestle
b) ghost, though, although, eight, weight, height, high,
thigh, knight, neighbour, neigh c) comb, bomb, tomb, climb,
limb, lamb d) glisten, hustle, wrestle, bristle, bustle, nestle,
rustle, thistle, whistle, trestle

**Spelling Week 15 – Words with Long and Short *oo*
Sounds, pp. 58–59**
1. a) scoop b) rooster c) brook d) wool e) shook f) cartoon g)
hood h) smoothie i) noodle j) stood

Spelling Week 15 – Word Study, p. 60
1. a) tuna, grew, glue b) true, drew, fruit c) loop, goose, clue
d) preview, soup, gloomy
2. a) stood, would, took b) wood, could, woof c) crook,
nook, bull d) foot, cookie, brook, soot
3. a) S b) N c) L d) L e) N f) S g) N h) S i) L

Spelling Week 15 – Word Study, p. 61
1.

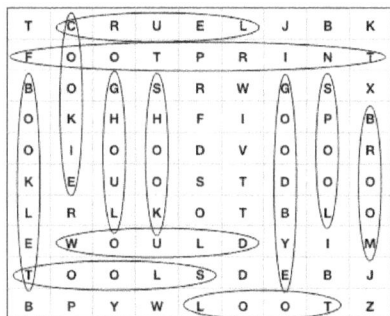

2. Sample answers: a) boot, route, suit, scoot, root b)
brook, took, look, hook, nook, shook
c) moon, soon, rune, prune, balloon, dune, goon, baboon,
spoon d) room, bloom, plume, tomb, womb e) full, wool,
bull, awful f) grew, blue, blew, knew, new, due, sue, flu, flew,
flue, true, shoo, shoe, glue, flue, flu g) pool, tool, cool, stool,
fool, rule, school h) could, good, would, stood, understood,
wood i) moose, goose, juice

Spelling Week 16 – Words with *oi* and *oy*, pp. 62–63
1. a) noisy b) asteroid c) choice d) destroy e) voyage f) loyal
g) moisture h) avoid i) oyster j) enjoy

Spelling Week 16 – Word Study, p. 64
1. a) avoid b) noisy c) loyal d) choice e) destroy f) voyage
2. a) board + walk, earth + worm b) down + pour, foot +
print, cheese + cake c) grape + vine, fire + place, corn +
stalk

Spelling Week 16 – Word Study, p. 65
1. a) enjoy b) oyster c) asteroid d) noisy e) avoid f) voyage g)
choice h) destroy i) loyal j) moisture
2. Sample answers: a) joint, point, coin, android, toilet, boil,
coil, spoil, soil, toil, voice, oink, noise b) joy, royal, toy, soy,
coy, boy, cowboy, gargoyle, ahoy, annoy, alloy, employ

Spelling Week 17 – Words with *ow* and *ou*, pp. 66–67
1. a) downtown b) outside c) allow d) cloudy e) announcer f)
browse g) compound h) coward
i) powerful j) pouch

Spelling Week 17 – Word Study, p. 68
1. a) underline: plough, crowd, allow; circle: although, glow
b) underline: sprout, aloud; circle: pillow, narrow, borrow c)
underline: grouch, cowl; circle: sparrow, snowball, shadow
d) underline: bounce, proud, shout; circle: throw, swallow
2. a) very top of a mountain b) sneak a quick look c) lend
something such as money or property d) solitary or single;
the only one e) sweet thick spread made from fruit and
sugar f) side surface of a doorway or window g) failed to
reach, hit, or some into contact with something aimed at
h) cloud of tiny water droplets in the air

Spelling Week 17 – Word Study, p. 69
1.

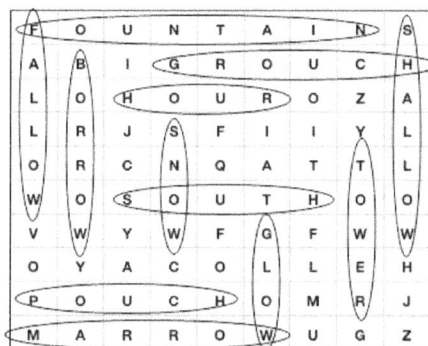

2. Sample answers: a) willow b) clown, down, town, drown,
crown c) sour, hour d) fowl, cowl, owl e) found, sound,
round, ground f) shower, power, tower g) south h) proud,
cloud i) mouse, grouse

**Spelling Week 18 – Words with an *s* Sound: c and s, pp.
70–71**
1. a) disaster b) practice c) delicious d) saucer e) process f)
pharmacy g) collapse h) exciting
i) absent j) unicycle

© Chalkboard Publishing Inc

Spelling Week 18 – Word Study, p. 72
1. a) organism, reason b) pose, wisdom, pause c) business, clothes, cookies d) prism, claws, present
2. a) nearby b) shut something c) someone being treated by a doctor d) able to tolerate or accept delays, problems, or suffering without becoming annoyed or anxious e) poor reason for having done something f) to lessen the blame for something g) happy h) what is in something **Note:** The order of the answers for c and d doesn't matter because the pair of words is identical. It is only important that children choose the correct definitions.

Spelling Week 18 – Word Study, p. 73
1.

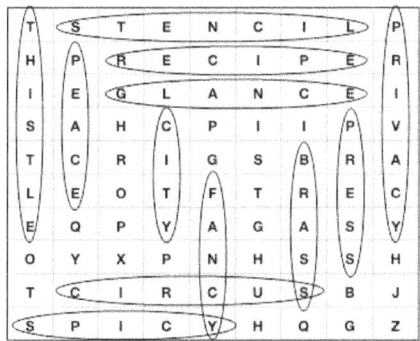

2. Sample answers: a) lift, gift, drift, shift, miffed b) mice, nice, spice, rice, dice, twice c) glance, lance, prance, ants, aunts d) list, missed, fist, mist e) mace, lace, face, race, pace, case, space, trace, grace, bass f) mess, bless, caress g) west, pest, messed, best, rest, nest, test h) loose, moose, goose, caboose i) cider, rider, strider, wider, divider, guider, collider

Spelling Week 19 – Words with a *j* Sound: g and j, pp. 74–75
1. a) reject b) mythology c) changing d) general e) journey f) magenta g) January h) adjust i) giant j) biology

Spelling Week 19 – Word Study, p. 76
1. a) angle, gift b) organize, finger c) garden, guard d) geese, wiggle
2. a) the study of crime and criminals b) the study of the Earth, its substance, history, and the processes that act on it c) the study of fossil animals and plants d) the study of the atmosphere to forecast the weather e) the study of volcanoes f) the study of birds g) the study of reptiles and amphibians h) the study of skin disorders

Spelling Week 19 – Word Study, p. 77
1. a) journey b) reject c) general d) changing e) mythology f) magenta g) adjust h) biology
i) January j) giant
2. Sample answers: a) jacket, jingle, jungle, jump, jive, jiggle b) fudge, nudge, budge, edge, ledge, age, rage, sage, dodge, danger, range, ranger, stranger c) ginseng, ginger, gigantic, digit, contagious, religion, religious d) smudgy, fudgy, edgy, spongy, strategy, technology, apology

Spelling Week 20 – Words with an *f* Sound Spelled *ph, gh,* and *f*, pp. 78–79
1. a) enough b) breakfast c) difficult d) drift e) autograph f) cliffs g) laughter h) rough i) cough
j) spherical

Spelling Week 20 – Word Study, p. 80
1. Sample answers: a) ice cubes; icicles b) firey orange ball; fireball c) perfume; heaven
d) warm hug; cozy blanket e) butterflies; fairies; dancers f) a wild horse; a raging lion g) crashing cymbals; drum rolls
2. a) scratchy b) strong
3. a) cry b) real

Spelling Week 20 – Word Study, p. 81
1.

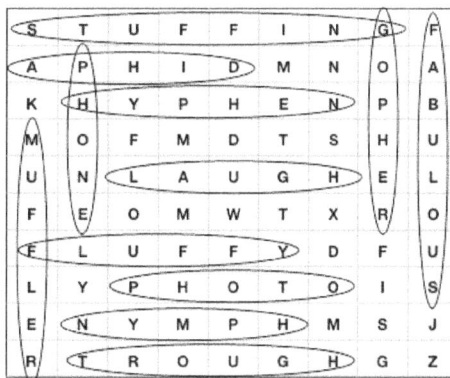

2. Sample answers: a) half, staff, graph b) tough, fluff, cuff, stuff, enough c) lake, rake, shake, brake, break, take, cake, sake, bake, wake, sake, ache, mistake, quake, earthquaked) meal, seal, wheel, congeal, reel, real, teal, squeal e) judge, grudge, smudge f) alone, shown, crone, blown, thrown g) linx, stinks, inks, sinks, rinks, minks, shrinks, slinks h) pinch, winch, cinch
i) smile, while, isle, aisle, style

Spelling Week 21 – Consonant Digraphs: *ch, sh, th,* and *wh*, pp. 82–83
1. a) whirls b) fashion c) thunder d) establish e) shadow f) exchange g) approach h) chimney
i) theatre j) whisper

Spelling Week 21 – Word Study, p. 84
1. a) lunch b) thought c) shingles d) fourth e) fish f) change g) throat h) whether i) thing j) whisper k) splash l) chimp
2. Sample answers: a) whip, ship, chip b) chick, thick c) wish, with d) chat, that, what e) then, when f) chin, shin, thin g) cheat, wheat h) chose, those, whose

Spelling Week 21 – Word Study, p. 85
1. a) whirl b) exchange c) thunder d) approach e) establihs f) fashion g) chimney h) shadow
i) theatre j) whisper

Spelling Week 22 – Consonant Blends: *scr, spl, spr,* and *str*, pp. 86–87
1. a) sprint b) astronaut c) sprig d) subscribe e) splinter f) describe g) instruction h) straight
i) instrument j) splatter

Spelling Week 22 – Word Study, p. 88
1. a) tuna, blew, true b) glue, crew, fruit c) pool, loose, due d) review, soup, loom
2. a) stood, could, look b) soot, should, woof c) hood, wood, pull d) cookie, brook, foot
3. a) S b) N c) L d) L e) N f) S g) N h) S i) L

Spelling Week 22 – Word Study, p. 89
1.

2. a) scrunch b) street c) spritz d) stream e) scrub f) splat g) script h) sprayer i) strength j) sprout k) stripes l) spread

Spelling Week 23 – *R*-controlled Vowels with *or, er, ir, ur,* and *ear*, pp. 90–91
1. a) sailor b) urban c) appear d) chapter e) pearl f) doctor g) adverb h) squirm i) thirsty j) urgent

Spelling Week 23 – Word Study, p. 92
1. Sample answers: a) whirr, fir, stir, sir; sire, fire, wire, tire, expire b) term, germ, fern c) blur, purr, sure, burst, burn, burp, during, fury, curl; bury, four, pour, course, court, source, lure
d) worm, world, word, worse, worst, work; born, torn, tore, sore, shore, more, sorry, four, for, fourteen e) learn, heard, pearl, early, earth, earthquake; bear, clear f) were; where, nowhere, here, mere, sphere, adhere, severe

2. a) aloud b) bury c) cent d) fowl e) groan f) knead g) lynx h) mane i) muscle j) patted k) paws
l) plane

Spelling Week 23 – Word Study, p. 93
1. a) urgent b) thirsty c) pearl d) appear e) squirm f) adverb g) urban h) chapter i) doctor j) sailor

Spelling Week 24 – *R*-controlled Vowels with *ar, are, or,* and *ore*, pp. 94–95
1. a) snore b) ignore c) flare d) apartment e) factor f) scared g) artist h) store i) aware j) editor

Spelling Week 24 – Word Study, p. 96
1. a) chore b) ignore c) park d) rare e) shark f) torn
2. You may wish to invite children to share some of their sentences with the class.

Spelling Week 24 – Word Study, p. 97
1.

2. Sample answers: a) score, swore, wore, store, shore, more b) lark, mark, ark, bark, park
c) worn, born, torn, morn d) mare, care, hair, hare, fair, fare, scare, share, spare, pear, bear, lair, stair, glare e) sport, court, port, sort, fort f) carp, harp g) ford, bored, award, lord, scored, sword, roared, gored, chord, cored h) ferret, merit i) fork, pork

Spelling Week 25 – Homographs and Homophones, pp. 98–99
1. a) wood b) there c) paws d) cent e) would f) their g) hire h) scent i) higher j) pause

Spelling Week 25 – Word Study, p. 100
1. a) rain or rein b) chews c) seen d) sighed e) steal f) peace g) herd h) stare i) yolk j) weave
k) very l) thrown
2. a) plump cooing birds with a small head, short legs b) plunged head first into water c) burning that gives off light, heat, and smoke d) let go from a job e) as good as possible f) to make something perfect g) air current blowing from a specific direction h) turn a key to operate a clockwork object **Note:** The order of the answers for c and d doesn't matter because the pair of words is identical. It is only important that children choose the correct definitions.

Spelling Week 25 – Word Study, p. 101
1.

2. a) take something without paying for it b) hard, strong grey or bluish metal c) attached or fastened with string or cord d) rising and falling of the sea with the moon and sun